GUITAR WORLD PRESENTS

GUITAR WORLD PRESENTS

STEVIE RAY VAUGHAN

FROM THE PAGES OF

GUITAR WORLD

MAGAZINE

Backbeat
Books

AN IMPRINT OF HAL LEONARD CORPORATION
NEW YORK

Published in 2010 by Backbeat Books
An Imprint of Hal Leonard Corporation
7777 West Bluemound Road
Milwaukee, WI 53213

Trade Book Division Editorial Offices
19 West 21st Street, New York, NY 10010

Printed in the United States of America

Executive Producer: Brad Tolinski
Editors: Jeff Kitts, Brad Tolinski, Chris Scapelliti
Art Director: Alexis Cook
Photo Editors: Jimmy Hubbard, Samantha Xu
Cover Photograph: Robert Knight

Library of Congress Cataloging-in-Publication data is available upon request.

ISBN 978-0-87930-971-8

www.backbeatbooks.com

CONTENTS

GUITAR WORLD PRESENTS

STEVIE RAY VAUGHAN

REPRINTED FROM *GUITAR WORLD*, APRIL 1999

[1]

"I would wake up and guzzle something, just to
**get rid of the pain
I was feeling.**"
—*STEVIE RAY VAUGHAN*

BLUE SMOKE:
THE LIFE AND DEATH OF
STEVIE RAY VAUGHAN

The explosive history of the man who
saved the blues and then himself—only to die
a tragic death. As told by Stevie Ray and his
closest friends and associates.

BY ALAN PAUL

TWENTY YEARS AFTER HIS DEATH, Stevie Ray Vaughan's influence only continues to grow. It can be heard in barrooms and arenas around the globe, in the playing of everyone from protégés like Kenny Wayne Shepherd to mentors like Buddy Guy to younger rockers like Joe Bonamassa and John Mayer. It can be seen in the popularity of vintage gear and straight-forward, ear-ringing tone, both of which were considered passé before Stevie proved that there was plenty of life left in Stratocasters and tube amps.

But perhaps the most telling statement about Stevie's continued relevance is that his music still speaks volumes to millions of listeners. Some voices are stilled by death, but his has only grown louder.

Editor's note: This article contains passages that appear elsewhere in this book.

"Unfortunately, you never fully grasp someone's greatness or importance until they're gone," says B.B. King. "And I think that's true with Stevie. As the years go by and he's not here, it just becomes more and more clear how special he was, and how much he's missed."

Missed so much that hungry fans eagerly await news of "lost" SRV tracks discovered in the vaults, crossing their fingers with the hope that a mother lode of unreleased material sits waiting to be unearthed and aired.

To understand what made Stevie tick, to get the whole story of the man behind the music, we turned to his closest confidantes, the people who knew him best and miss him the most. Given the opportunity to tell Stevie's tale, they opened up, revealing things they'd never revealed before. The result is a portrait of an artist completely dedicated to his craft, and of a man who had wrestled with his demons and emerged victorious, with a new lease on life and a rededicated passion for his life's work. Stevie Ray was undoubtedly making the finest music of his life when he died at age 35. This is his story, as told by his best friends and biggest heroes—and the one soul best qualified to do so: himself.

You know the music. Now meet the man.

CAST OF CHARACTERS

(IN ORDER OF APPEARANCE)

STEVIE RAY VAUGHAN Blues guitar great. Born October 3, 1954, Dallas, Texas. Died August 27, 1990, East Troy, Wisconsin. All quotes taken from *Guitar World* interviews

JIMMIE VAUGHAN Stevie Ray's older brother and primary guitar influence

DOYLE BRAMHALL Songwriting partner and longtime friend and bandmate

TOMMY SHANNON Double Trouble bass player

DENNY FREEMAN Guitarist, fellow Dallas native, bandmate of both Stevie and Jimmie

DR. JOHN New Orleans blues pianist/guitarist, and SRV friend

B.B. KING King of the blues. Godfather to all blues guitarists

RAY HENNIG Owner of Heart of Texas music shop; sold Stevie his "Number One" Strat

ANGELA STREHLI Austin blues singer; taught Stevie "Texas Flood"

WC CLARK Austin guitarist who played bass in and co-fronted the Triple Threat Revue with Stevie and singer Lou Ann Barton

CHRIS LAYTON Double Trouble drummer

BONNIE RAITT Slide guitar diva and close friend of SRV

ERIC CLAPTON British blues guitar great, friend and admirer of SRV

DICKEY BETTS Allman Brothers Band guitarist

REESE WYNANS Double Trouble keyboardist

JIM GAINES *In Step* producer

BUDDY GUY Chicago blues guitar legend, friend of and hero to SRV

IN THE BEGINNING

STEVIE RAY VAUGHAN I got my first guitar when I was seven. It was one of those Roy Rogers guitars; it had pictures of cowboys and cows on it, some rope. I had a blanket that had the same shit on it, too. When I was real young, [*western swing band*] the Texas Playboys hung out at our house all the time. My parents played "42" [*dominoes*], and they'd come over and get drunk. Those guys hung around a lot, they'd do some playing, and we'd hear their stuff. Mainly, we'd hear them talking about it. There were a lot of *characters* hanging around. Every once in a while, my dad would yell [*affects heavy rural Texas accent*], "Hey, Jim, Steve, come out here and show them what you can do!" And we were little midgets, with guitars hangin' on us that were this big!

JIMMIE VAUGHAN I went straight for the blues, because that's what sounded best to me; I can't tell you why. It spoke to me more than country, which was the other thing I heard all the time. A lot of my relatives were country musicians, and I never even tried to play country. All my relatives looked at me like, "What in the world are you doing?" but I just said, "I like *this*." And I never thought about it again.

SRV When we started off, I knew how Jimmy Reed sounded, but I couldn't play it right. And Jimmie would set me straight. A lot of the time, I just watched him play. Jimmie turned me on to a lot of different stuff. I remember several different things: him bringing home records by Hendrix, Buddy Guy, Muddy Waters, B.B. King. The first record I ever bought was "Wham," by Lonnie Mack, from 1963, which was a great record. I played it so many times, my dad got mad and broke it! When I didn't think it could be any louder, I went and borrowed somebody's Shure Vocal Master P.A., put mikes in front of the stereo speakers, and turned the P.A. up! It was *loud* in my room.

JIMMIE VAUGHAN When we were real little, my dad had a job which required him to travel around the South, and we all trailed around. It was real tough—going to schools for two weeks at a time, always uprooting. In a way, it was perfect training for the life we eventually lived as musicians, on the road all the time. Then we settled back in Dallas, when I was in first grade, in Oak Cliff, which was a real rough place. Pretty much everyone we grew up with is either dead or in jail. And I think we latched onto the guitar as a way out pretty early on. The guitar took Stevie around the world. It introduced him to his heroes. It was his instrument of liberation, his magic sword. It meant everything; I can't even fathom Stevie without a guitar. It allowed him to express himself like never before, to have an identity. When Stevie played, his guitar literally talked. If you listen, you can hear it. You can hear *him* speaking through his guitar. I showed him the way initially, but he found his voice himself.

SRV Jimmie showed me a lot of stuff, but there was also a time when he warned, "If you ask me to show you anything again, I'll kick your ass." Well, I did and he did.

DOYLE BRAMHALL Jimmie and I were in a band called the Chessmen together when we were teenagers in Dallas. He was 15 and I was 17, so I could drive and he couldn't, and I would go by and pick him up. One time—this was sometime in 1966—he wasn't ready so he waved me in. I was sitting in the living room, waiting, and Jimmie walked from the back bedroom to the kitchen and I heard this guitar playing going on from the other direction. I walked down the hall and a bedroom door was a little ajar. I looked and there was this little skinny 12-year-old kid sitting on the bed, playing Jeff Beck's "Jeff's Boogie." As soon as he saw me, he stopped playing and I said, "Don't stop." He gave me this shy little smile and said, "Hi, I'm Stevie," and I said, "Hi. I'm Doyle. Keep playing. You're very good." Thirty seconds later, Jimmie ran up and said, "Let's go."

"I saw this scrawny little 14- or 15-year-old kid **just wailing away. It was Stevie.**"
—*TOMMY SHANNON*

TOMMY SHANNON In 1969, I was playing with Johnny Winter, did Woodstock and everything. When we broke up, I flew back to Dallas and one day dropped by this club called the Fog, where I had met Johnny. I walked in and heard this unbelievable guitar player. A bunch of people were talking to me and I just ignored them 'cause I was looking to see who was making this big sound. I looked up and saw this scrawny little 14- or 15-year-old kid just wailing away. It was Stevie. He was real awkward and shy and looking up at the big guys around him, really intimidated. In fact, he said once in an interview that I was the only one who would talk to him, and I told him the truth. I said, "You're already better than all these guys." He gave me a big smile and we made friends right then and there.

DENNY FREEMAN Jimmie and Stevie were both better than most people ever get the first time I heard them play—when they were 16 or 17.

BRAMHALL There was really only one place in Dallas, the Cellar, where you could play Muddy Waters on 10. So in about 1970, Jimmie and I and a bunch of other guys decided to move to Austin, where there were more places to play and it was cheaper to live. It was like a little San Francisco; you could come down here and express yourself, and people left you alone to do your thing. We started having a little scene, and about a year later, Stevie moved there with his band, Blackbird.

I was still playing with Jimmie, doing mostly straight blues, but Stevie and I both wanted to branch out a little more. We were listening to people like Marvin Gaye and Sly Stone and wanted to incorporate some of that stuff into our music, so Stevie and I found each other getting together more often. In late '72, he called me up and told me that he had gotten a phone call from Marc Benno, who had a deal with A&M and a big tour lined up, and needed to put together a Texas blues-rock band to do it. We went out to L.A. to record, and it was a new kick for us just to be out of Texas. Other than little trips to Oklahoma or Louisiana, I don't think any of us had even left the state.

We were in L.A. for two weeks, riding around in limos and living like rock stars. We recorded seven songs—including "Dirty Pool," which was the first song Stevie and I wrote together—and three of them are actually good, and should be heard. Then we went on a short tour with Humble Pie and the J. Geils Band. We played seven or eight gigs in places like Detroit, Chicago and New York, and it was our first time out in the big world. Unfortunately, however, music took a back seat to drinking and drugging—especially for me—so while we played some good music, it was pretty much a mess, and I guess the label hated it. So we ended up back in Austin and decided to keep the band together, as the Nightcrawlers. That lasted a while, and when it fell apart, Stevie went back to California for a while, then came back and joined Paul Ray and the Cobras, with Denny Freeman.

FREEMAN I was the Cobras' sole guitar player before Stevie joined, so it was a little tough to have him join. But it was also really exciting to play with him.

DR. JOHN Stevie had this real boyish charm. He kept this very appealing childhood innocence about him—even when he wasn't innocent at all.

B.B. KING He reminded me of my sons when they were about seven or eight years old. He just had so many questions, and would just follow me around, happy and smiling and eager to please.

FREEMAN Stevie almost didn't talk about anything except guitars and music. He was just completely obsessed with it, and so was I. Those were just fun, exciting days because we were just discovering stuff and were excited about everything, and we would just sit around for hours talking about music.

RAY HENNIG I've owned a guitar store since 1960 and have seen a lot of great musicians, but I don't believe I've ever come across anyone half as obsessed with the guitar as Stevie was. He used to hang out in my store, just noodling on guitars all the time. I would say that he was one of my best customers, except he didn't have any money—he was broke all the time—so he never paid for anything in those days. He used to come by on his way to a gig and ask for a pack of strings. I'd toss him one and he'd say, "Hey, if I make any money tonight, I'll pay you." And he would. I lent him guitars all the time. He'd take them for a week or two, then bring them back.

One day in '74, he brought back a nice Strat he had been borrowing and was looking through all the instruments when he came to his ol' beater. He picked it up and must have played around with it for half an hour, just making chords, turning it over, looking at it, weighing it, before he asked if he could plug it in. I said, "Sure, but it sure is ugly." So he plugged in and played for an hour or so then told me he wanted it, and asked if he could swap it for the one he had just returned. I said, "Well, you're ripping yourself off. That has got to be cheesiest Strat I've ever traded for. It's raggedy-assed and beat to death. What do you want it for?" He said, "It just feels good, Ray. It feels real good." I figured he'd bring it back in a day or two, but he never did. That became his "Number One" Strat.

THE TRIPLE THREAT REVUE

FREEMAN Stevie was already great when he joined the Cobras. In fact, our drummer just sent me a tape of some sides we cut, and his lead playing sounds fantastic—and immediately identifiable as Stevie. He maybe wasn't as strong a rhythm player as he would become, and didn't understand chord changes that well yet, but his lead playing was *there*. When he decided to leave and front his own band, which became Triple Threat Revue, it wasn't surprising. He was ready, and it was obvious to all of us that he had some sort of destiny.

ANGELA STREHLI I was doing "Texas Flood" for years. And when he decided to start a group, to become a frontman, he knew that he really should be singing. And he came to me, said that he always liked "Texas Flood," and asked if I could teach him the words, which I did. He needed some encouragement to sing; he was still a little scared. But he took the song and made it so associated with him that I quit doing it, because, after a while, everyone thought I was imitating him.

WC CLARK I was working at McMorris Ford as a mechanic, and Stevie kept coming by and telling me that he'd decided to put a band together and that he needed me to play bass. I wasn't looking for a gig, because I was getting a steady paycheck and relaxing for a change, but he kept pestering me. I had seen him around a lot, and I knew how unique he was—how clean a tone he had, how nasty and lowdown he could be, how he could play licks exactly like Chuck Berry, Albert King and B.B. King. I knew he was for real, that he was a seeker, a warrior. And that's why I not only agreed to join his band, but to play bass for him, even though I had given up the instrument to focus on guitar. I really had no interest in playing bass again, but Stevie had such a fire, and I was so impressed by how much he had already improved, that I wanted to see where he could take it. So I joined what became the Triple Threat Review.

DR. JOHN My friend Doc Pomus [*composer of such R&B classics as "This Magic Moment" and "Save the Last Dance for Me"*] kept telling me about this Texas guitar player I had to come to see at the Lone Star Cafe in Manhattan. Stevie was still playing with Lou Ann [*Barton*] and he was a hell of a good guitar player, but wasn't really special yet. He was just playing in a Houston style à la Pat Hare,

Wayne Bennett and Albert Collins. A year or so later, I saw him again and noticed how much this kid had blossomed. He had gotten this whole Albert King bending thing down stone cold and his playing had just taken off. I thought anyone who improved so much so fast had something going on.

LAYTON I started playing with Stevie right after WC Clark left the band in '78. The band was no longer a "triple threat," so Stevie changed the name to Double Trouble, after the Otis Rush song. The next fall we got booked to play at the San Francisco Blues Festival. I helped book all these gigs around that, and none of them paid more than 200 bucks. We had only enough money to buy gas for the van and loaves of bread and bologna. We couldn't afford to eat a square meal, but it was a lot of fun. We played the Festival, and we did a live radio broadcast on KFAG, in Palo Alto, where we opened up for Robert Cray, who was starting to have a big name on the circuit out there. We became good friends with him, and we started to make a name for ourselves, get a little buzz, because anyone who saw Stevie wondered who the hell he was. About a year later, Lou Ann left and we became just a trio with me and Jackie Newhouse playing behind Stevie.

SHANNON In December 1980, I was living in Houston and went to see Double Trouble when they were in town; it was like a revelation. I said, "That's where I belong, right there." He called me up to jam, and soon after asked me if I wanted to join. His guitar playing had come a long way, and he had crossed the gap from straight blues, incorporating some rock and roll, some Hendrix. He was a little scared to step out of the blues, and I really encouraged him. He got some shit from the blues purists for that, but who cares? Being a purist is like being a religious fundamentalist. It's really limiting, and if you can't see beyond the little circle you draw around yourself, how are you gonna move out of it? And anyhow, he never, ever abandoned the blues; he just advanced it, took it to another level.

DR. JOHN Stevie started really blowing me away one night when we were hanging at his pad. He put on some trippy, difficult Hendrix album and started playing along with it, which impressed me. Then he started playing off it, getting down, improvising and I thought, Man, this kid is jamming with Jimi Hendrix. That's when I saw something real unique in what he was going for and realized that this guy was something altogether different.

BONNIE RAITT Just when you thought there wasn't any other way to make this stuff your own, he came along and blew that theory to bits. Soul is an overused word, but the fire and passion with which he invested everything he touched was just astounding, as was the way in which he synthesized his influences and turned them into something so fiercely personal. I was amazed from the first time I saw him, but I had already heard all about him from guys like Albert Collins and Buddy Guy, who kept running into him and being blown away.

LAYTON Stevie never failed to impress, and that finally started to pay off in a tangible way in late '81. First, our manager somehow got a video of a show to Mick Jagger, and the next thing we knew we were playing a private party for the Rolling Stones in New York. That was a gas. Then Lou Ann Barton had a solo record coming out on a major label and we played at the big release party at the Continental Club. [*Veteran A&R man and producer*] Jerry Wexler, who had signed her, was there, and he really liked us and called up his friend, Claude Nobs, at the Montreux Jazz Festival and got us booked there. We were supposedly the first unsigned band to ever play it, and lots of good things happened as a result.

David Bowie was in the audience and he was blown away by Stevie, called him the best urban blues player he'd ever heard. He came back to the hotel and we all hung out in the bar with him for an hour. He told Stevie that he was going to be doing a bluesy record and asked him if he'd like to be on it. Stevie said, "Sure, give me a call." Meanwhile, the next night we booked ourselves into that same bar. We played all night, and Jackson Browne and his whole band came and sat in with us. We jammed until seven A.M., and then Jackson said he had a pre-production studio in L.A., Down Town, and that any time we wanted to come record some tracks free of charge, we were welcome.

TEXAS FLOOD

LAYTON I don't think Jackson expected us to take him up on his offer, but Stevie called him in the fall, and he agreed to give us 72 hours of free time over Thanksgiving weekend '82. We went up there, just hoping that maybe we were making a demo that would actually be listened to by a real record company. It turned out that, without knowing it, we were recording our debut album, *Texas Flood*. We just rolled in. The guys working there were mildly annoyed because it was Thanksgiving weekend, and we were like, "Hey, uh, you guys got any tape?" They gave us some used stuff; we actually recorded over some of Jackson's demos for *Lawyers in Love*.

SHANNON Down Town was really just a big warehouse with concrete floors and some rugs thrown down. We found a little corner, set up in a circle looking at and listening to each other and played like a live band. We didn't really do anything the first day, then we cut two songs the second day and eight the third. The last tune we cut was "Texas Flood," right before our time ran out.

LAYTON We stayed in L.A. and played a few dates, and one night at three in the morning the phone rang in our apartment, and this guy with an English accent asked for Stevie. I said he was sleeping and asked who it was. "It's David Bowie," he said, "and I'd like to speak to him if possible." I got Stevie up and Bowie asked him if he wanted to come to New York and cut some tracks for his new record.

SHANNON Stevie went and did it and enjoyed it, and said Bowie was a real gentleman. The feelings were obviously mutual because he asked Stevie to join his band for a world tour. Stevie finally agreed because he was getting a lot of pressure from a lot of people. Stevie was going to do it for a year, take the money and pay us to keep the band together. Then he asked Bowie if we could open some dates, and that was supposed to happen, then fell through. And then Stevie was told that he couldn't mention his own band or music in interviews, and that was it. He quit the night before the tour was supposed to start. He just couldn't do it because it wasn't what he loved playing. He liked David and his music, but it wasn't where he was headed and Stevie could not do what he didn't love.

LAYTON I wasn't surprised when Stevie quit, but I sure was happy. I couldn't believe that just when we seemed to have all this momentum, Stevie was going to be gone for at least a year, maybe more. We had worked so hard to get to that point, where it seemed like something was going to happen, that I just figured that, somehow, the whole thing would not come to pass. Then, sure enough, we found out that John Hammond really liked our tape, and was pushing to get us signed by Columbia. All of a sudden, we had a deal with Epic and they were going to release *Texas Flood*. And we got more attention because people wanted to know who this unknown guy who told David Bowie to take a hike was. And his playing on *Let's Dance* got people's attention, too.

ERIC CLAPTON Stevie was one of three or four artists who I heard and had to know who it was, right then. I was driving and "Let's Dance" came on the radio. I stopped my car and said, "I have to know who this guitar player is today. Not tomorrow, but today."

SHANNON *Texas Flood* came out and we started touring behind it. We could slowly feel things changing, the crowds slowly getting bigger and bigger. Then we got rid of the milk truck we had been driving around in and got a bus. It was a really shitty bus, but we were in heaven riding around in it.

LAYTON We toured the whole country, playing every night, selling out 500-seat clubs, with 200 people standing outside trying to get in. And all of a sudden, "Pride and Joy" was being played on MTV, and it was just unreal.

DICKEY BETTS When I heard "Pride and Joy" on the radio, I said "hallelujah." Stevie Ray Vaughan single-handedly brought guitar- and blues-oriented music back to the marketplace. He was just so good and strong that he would not be denied.

COULDN'T STAND THE WEATHER / SOUL TO SOUL

LAYTON We went to New York to record our second album and it was a kick, because we were staying at the Mayflower Hotel and recording at the Power Station, produced by John Hammond, who had discovered everyone from Charlie Christian to Bruce Springsteen and Bob Dylan. And we had a real budget to work with for the first time. We were all doing our fair share of drugs and partying, but it wasn't hurting us yet. We were pretty good at all of it about that time.

SRV We ran into Clapton on a tour of Australia. He was leaving the hotel and I went out to talk to him, hangover and all. He was sober, of course, and really calm while I sat there downing two or three shots of Crown Royal. And he just sort of looked at me wisely and said, "Well, sometimes you have to go through that, don'tcha?" If I had been ready to stop, he would have gone on to the next part—but he understood that I wasn't.

Another time we were doing a show with Albert King, and he walked backstage and said, "We gonna have a little heart to heart. I been watching you wrestle with the bottle three, four times already. I tell you what, man: I like to drink a little bit when I'm home. But the gig ain't no time to get high." He was trying to tell me to take care of business, give myself a break, but I did my usual deal of trying to act like I had it all together: "Hey, ain't nuthin' wrong, man, I'm leading the life," and all that bullshit.

"I think *Soul to Soul* is a good record but you can kind of tell that **we're a little out of sorts.**"

—*TOMMY SHANNON*

SHANNON By the time we got to recording *Soul to Soul* in '85, it was getting pretty bad. We were paying for the studio time and spending hours upon hours playing ping pong waiting for our cocaine to arrive before we'd play. I think *Soul to Soul* is a good record but you can kind of tell that we're a little out of sorts.

REESE WYNANS When they were recording *Soul to Soul*, Stevie called and said they wanted me to come add some keyboards. They wanted me to play acoustic piano on "Look at Little Sister," but it didn't really work because they had such a strange setup. The studio was set up like a live performance, with an entire P.A. and all the amps and mics running through it. It was screaming loud and you could not hear a piano, so I suggested that we try a Hammond organ, where I could isolate the cabinet. We played "Change It" and the instrumentals, and it went great. We ended up recording until seven in the morning and they asked me to come back the next night. The guys told me they were glad I came over, because they had been having a hard time getting the project off the ground. Then Stevie asked me if I wanted to join the band.

LAYTON We were in a bit of a drug and alcohol frenzy by then, and when you go into the studio you have to confront what you really sound like. You can't just walk off the stage and have it over and done with; you're under a microscope. *Soul to Soul* came out well, but it was very difficult to make, and I think that had a lot to do with asking Reese to join. It was like, "We need some help here," somebody to help carry everything. We had actually added another guitarist, Derek O'Brien, who's just wonderful, for a few shows, but our manager felt that took the spotlight away from Stevie. And a lot of people were urging us to keep the trio thing, but we really needed a new perspective. We had been on an endless three-year tour punctuated by time in the studio, and we were getting burnt.

But Stevie was continuing to stretch out, trying different tones and weird stuff. We used to call him "Modern Man" because he loved to fool around with electronics, take things apart and put them back together, and he loved to just try crazy stuff. Like on "Ain't Gone 'N' Give Up on Love," Stevie took a six-string bass and put paper matches under the bridge saddle to muffle the sound—and that's what you hear on the little strum on the downbeat. We would get crazy ideas after we had been up too long and our minds were racing. Suddenly, you go, "I wonder what I would get if I put a half-cut Coke can under my bass drum pedal." And sometimes those things would actually work.

WYNANS Business-wise, I was just shocked by what was going on with them—or not going on. They were so successful as a band, I assumed their business was in order. But they didn't even know how much money they had. And the drugging was getting so bad that I was really scared for the guys' health. Stevie was just so worn down, he obviously needed a rest, but it's hard to stop working when you find out you're in big debt. So we stayed out there and got worse and worse, and probably reached sort of a low point at some of the shows we were recording for *Live Alive*.

FREEMAN I was at the gigs they recorded at the Austin Opera House [*July 17–18, 1986*]. I hadn't seen them in a while, and I really was disturbed by what I saw. I thought, This is a musical mess, because they would go into these chaotic jams with no control. I didn't know what exactly was going on, but I was concerned.

SHANNON I remember sitting backstage at the Opera House and saying to our manager, Alex Hodges, "Stevie and I are headed for a brick wall." I saw it coming, but neither of us could stop—and we tried. Stevie knew he was in trouble, too, because we were really getting pathetic.

SRV I had been trying to pull myself up by the bootstraps, but they were broken. I would wake up and guzzle something, just to get rid of the pain I was feeling. Whiskey, beer, vodka, whatever was handy. It got to the point where if I'd try to say "Hi" to somebody, I would just fall apart crying. It was like...solid doom.

WYNANS Stevie and Tommy were just completely out of control when we did those Opera House shows, and it was getting scary. The first year I was in the band, I saw people who were abusing substances, but also were on top of it musically. But that started to change. Things were getting illogical and crazy, and Stevie would sometimes play himself into corners and not know how the hell he was going to get out.

SRV God, I wasn't in very good shape when we recorded that. At the time, I didn't realize how bad a shape I was in. There were more fix-it jobs done on the album than I would have liked. There were some good nights and some good gigs, but it was more haphazard than we would have liked. Some of the gigs were okay, but some of them sound like they were the work of half-dead people. Of course, my thinking was, Boy, doesn't that sound good? And there were some great notes that came out, but I just wasn't in control; nobody was. We were all exhausted.

LAYTON It really had gotten silly. We were just trudging along, wondering if we would make it until the afternoon. It was like being in the middle of the desert, wondering if the next step would be the one where we just fell over and died.

SHANNON Stevie and I always had adjoining rooms on the road, and we'd leave the door between us open so it was like one big room. We went on a European tour, and were at a hotel in Germany. I was lying on my bed, sick as a dog, and I could see Stevie rolling around his bed mumbling shit, and just sticking his head over and vomiting blood all over the floor, too weak to get up and walk to the bathroom. There wasn't much I could to do to help him because I was so sick myself, but I went over. He was gray, so I called an ambulance and they came and got him.

LAYTON There were all these guys in white trench coats yelling in German and sticking IVs into Stevie; it was really scary. He went to the hospital and then we went to Zurich, Switzerland, and performed the next night, but Stevie sounded weak, both as a player and a person. I called our manager and said, "We have to do something." We were on our way to England, so I suggested that we call Dr. Bloom, who had helped Pete Townshend and Eric Clapton in similar situations. Stevie went there for a few days of rest, after which we did two shows in London. Before the second night encore, when we were walking back to the stage, Stevie walked onto this goofy gangplank at the back corner of the stage and fell off it. That was the straw that broke the camel's back, and he just said, "I'm too tired, I need rest and I need change." So we cancelled the rest of the tour and he went to a rehab clinic in Atlanta. It was a relief, really. I remember thinking, The whirlwind has finally stopped. And we're alive.

WYNANS Something had to give, and what gave was Stevie. He just had a breakdown, and it was a huge relief knowing that he was he was going to get some help.

SHANNON Stevie went to the Charter Lane treatment center in Atlanta and I went into one in Austin. We were both there 28 days, and that was just the beginning of the day-to-day process.

JIMMIE VAUGHAN It didn't even occur to me that Stevie would really go clean. I figured that he'd just do his 28 days to get everyone off his back, then go back to it. But he was serious, and dedicated, and he showed the way for me, and a lot of other people.

RAITT I was playing in Atlanta at the end of his rehab stay, and he came to see me. I invited him onstage, as we would always do for one another. I found out later that he was really nervous because it was his first time playing sober. But he played great, and there went my last excuse for not getting sober.

SRV The music has become really important [*since I've become sober*]. Music is a way to reach out and hold on to one another in a really healthy way. It's helped me to open up more and take a chance on loving people. It's a whole new world for me. More so than ever, if I don't play the best I possibly can, and really try to play better than I think I can, then I've wasted it. Because I'm playing on borrowed time. Left to my own devices, I would have killed myself. But for some reason I'm not dead.

IN STEP

LAYTON It was sort of a cruel irony that *Live Alive* came out right when Tommy and Stevie got out of treatment. One of the first times we got together again was to make a video for "Superstition." So everyone was clear-headed and healthy, and we were trying to play along to this dope- and booze-laden tune. It was like, "God, can't we cut this song again?" It was a weird contrast, but it was a great feeling to have everyone really into it again, ready to put the whole thing back together. It was the start of something real good.

WYNANS Stevie was real nervous about playing his first sober shows, but we hit the stage and it was just magical. Within three nights, he completely hit his stride and was playing better than any of us had ever heard him. He was playing the way he always wanted to and was just ecstatic. Every song was exciting, and ideas were constantly popping up and flowering everywhere.

CLAPTON He seemed to be an open channel. The music just poured through him, and it never dried up.

BRAMHALL Stevie and I got together to write songs for his new album, what became *In Step*, and did what we always did: spend a few days just hanging out talking and catching up, which would point us in the direction we were going to head. We had both sobered up within four months, and we knew that was something we had to deal with. It was important for us to talk about and write about our experiences with addiction. We wanted to directly confront the issues that surrounded our drug and alcohol days, which led to songs like "Wall of Denial" and "Tightrope."

SRV I was afraid that I'd turn people off, but somewhere along the way that quit mattering. It seems real important to me to write about that stuff. I had spent so long with this image of, "I'm cooler than so and so because I get higher than he does." And it's just not true.

LAYTON We went to Memphis to start recording *In Step* in the fall of '88, and it was very tedious at first. There was some trepidation because we knew it was our proving ground, that we had to show that we could make good records without anyone being high. I know Stevie felt the doubt. I think it ended up producing the tightest band performances of our career, but we really worked at it.

SHANNON Stevie would do anything to get new, different or better sounds, trying to wire different amps together or whatever, and he seemed to spend a lot of time messing with stuff on *In Step*. But his actual playing just flowed once he got down to it.

JIM GAINES Stevie told me he had an instrumental called "Riviera Paradise" he wanted to try, and I said that I only had nine minutes of tape left. He said, "Don't worry. It's only four minutes long." We dimmed the lights and they started playing this gorgeous song, which went on to six minutes, seven minutes, seven and a half... The song is absolutely incredible, totally inspired, dripping with emotion—and here we were, about to run out of tape. I was jumping up and down, waving my arms, but everyone was so wrapped up in their playing that no one was paying me any mind. I finally got Chris' attention and emphatically gave him the cut sign. He started trying to flag down Stevie, but he was hunched over his guitar with his head bent down. Finally, he looked up, and they brought the song down just in time. It ended and, a few seconds later, the tape finished and the studio was silent except for the sound of the empty reel spinning around. We cut the song a few more times, but it sounded like Muzak compared to that first, magical version.

SHANNON We finished the record and were really happy with it. Then we went back on the road, and it was a whole new world. The music was great, we had a great organization, a great road manager, Skip Rickert, a great crew. We were all just really happy, and Stevie was so great, it was just frightening. I never got used to playing with Stevie. I never took it for granted. It was like, "Okay, where the hell is he going tonight because I got to follow." Stevie never said, "Now play this." He just played and we followed, and it only got more and more exciting.

LAYTON We toured through the winter of '90, then took a break for Stevie to go record *Family Style* with Jimmie.

SHANNON Stevie really enjoyed cutting *Family Style* and spending all that time with his brother. He said it was like coming home. After they did that he took a little vacation and then we got back together to finish some touring. We ended the summer tour with the two shows at Alpine Valley, outside Chicago. It involved playing with Clapton and Robert Cray, and Jimmie and Buddy Guy came up to be special guests. It was just great fun, really exciting. Sort of the culmination of all the good times we'd been having for the last year or two. And, as good as we had been playing, those two shows were just unreal.

JIMMIE VAUGHAN Stevie just *smoked*. It was one of those gigs where you see someone play and you can't believe what you're hearing. They're just wailing and happy and making it happen, raising it another notch. That's what it was like that night at Alpine Valley. Stevie was unreal. He was just on another plane, and we all knew it.

RAITT The first night at Alpine Valley I was there just to watch, and it was just great to see everyone. I really think that Stevie was perhaps the greatest guitarist ever, and he just showed it that night.

BUDDY GUY Man, first of all, Stevie was one of the best ever. Period. But those nights, he was just something else. And I remember standing with him on the side of the stage while Eric was playing, and he was sort of playing air guitar, fingering along with what Eric played. After he died, for some reason I kept thinking of that, him standing there playing phantom notes.

SHANNON The first night I stuck around for the jam at the end, but the second night I wanted to get back to Chicago, so I took a helicopter back with Reese. I went to sleep and got woken up by a phone call from our tour manager at 6:30 A.M. He said that we had to have a meeting in my room right away. I said, "It's 6:30 in the morning, no time for a meeting. What the hell is going on?" And he said, "It's very important." I started feeling very uneasy, and a few minutes later I got a call from our manager, Alex Hodges, saying that one of the helicopters had gone down and Stevie was on it, and there were no survivors. In the blink of an eye my life was taken away from me. I was sitting on the bed, crying, and Chris came into my room, asking what was going on. I said, "Stevie's dead," and he just lost it, too.

LAYTON I was in denial, didn't believe it at all, so I called security and I forced them to let me into Stevie's room. I really thought he'd be there sleeping, but when they opened the door, the bed was still made and I just realized, "My God, it's true."

SHANNON Stevie's coat was laid out on the bed and, oddly, the clock radio was playing that Eagles song that goes, "And I may never see you again." It was playing real softly, but it might as well have been a bullhorn into my ear. Then we all went back to my room, and Jimmie was there, and we were all a wreck, sobbing and dazed. It was the most horrible moment in my life. I'll never have anything hurt that bad again, ever.

LAYTON I felt like a car had fallen on me or something. I felt like a baby, just completely helpless. Then we remembered that the news reports said that Stevie *and his band* were killed, and I realized that I had to get a hold of my family and tell them that I was still alive. So we spent a bunch of time calling our families, and just sort of going on autopilot. Because if I started thinking about it, I wouldn't be able to function.

DR. JOHN I played at his funeral which was really gut-wrenching. I played every hymn I knew, then Stevie Wonder came up and said to me, "Ave Marie in G," and I don't know it in any key. So I just stopped and let him sing a cappella, and once I wasn't playing, I got really aware. "Man, I'm with his coffin," and went into that zone, where it was all hitting me like gangbusters. Being in that little church and realizing that Stevie's feet were just a few feet away from me was so damn heavy I could hardly breathe.

FREEMAN You know, since Stevie died, he's been elevated to sainthood. It sounds strange, but in a weird way I think it diminishes him, because Stevie wasn't a saint. He was a person, and he had faults, but he was sweet and funny and a wonderful guy to hang with in addition to being an exceptional talent.

JIMMIE VAUGHAN The world misses his music, but I miss my brother.

[2]

"I was gifted with music for a reason, and it wasn't just to get famous."
—*STEVIE RAY VAUGHAN*

AUSTIN POWERHOUSE

The first printed interview ever conducted
with the young Stevie Ray Vaughan.

BY BILL BENTLEY

BACK IN THE LATE SEVENTIES, before he rose to national prominence, Stevie Ray Vaughan was a rising star in the thriving Austin, Texas, blues scene. As lead guitarist of the Triple Threat Revue, Stevie caught the attention of local journalist Bill Bentley, who quickly recognized that Vaughan was a "blues boy in the first degree." On April 28, 1978, Bentley conducted the first printed interview with the guitar superstar-in-the-making for the *Austin Sun*, a local weekly entertainment magazine. The following exquisitely captures the artist as a young blues man.

AUSTIN SUN When did you first start playing the guitar?

STEVIE RAY VAUGHAN Around 1964. I was in a band when I was 12 or 13. Then, in late '68, I heard a tape of Albert King and decided to dedicate myself to the blues. Listening to the great bluesmen—how they played so well and were so relaxed—really inspired me. I'm still trying to play that way. I'll probably pursue that the rest of my life.

AUSTIN SUN What was it like to be so young and playing clubs around Texas?

VAUGHAN I didn't understand a lot of it. Some of it went past me, but it was incredible.

AUSTIN SUN You grew up in Dallas but moved to Austin.

VAUGHAN You can't play blues in Dallas unless you're from out of town. All the musicians we know there are playing disco, or something like that. Austin is unique, in a way. Any night of the week you can go out and hear just about anything. People are out in the clubs.

"I heard a tape of Albert King and decided to **dedicate myself to the blues.**"
—STEVIE RAY VAUGHAN

AUSTIN SUN Austin seems to support their musicians.

VAUGHAN Yeah. There are lots of musicians try-ing to show people some kind of truth. All the musicians around here who work to be true to what they're doing, they're gifted with some-thing and it's like they're giving it back. Somebody has got to care.

So many times, though, it's like the masses of people are getting told what they're going to like next. Promoters saying, "This is the next thing, and you're going to dig it."

AUSTIN SUN What's your reward?

VAUGHAN There's a lot of them, but one stands out. When you're playing and all of the sudden you realize your toes are...just...tightened up, and you get a chill all the way up your back because of what you just gave somebody and what they gave back to you. That's probably the biggest thrill. Or, you're playing someplace and you just hit a note and people start screaming—that's it. You gave them a thrill, or you soothed them. That's what the blues do to me. If people tell me they don't want to hear a blues band because it brings them down, they're not paying attention at all. I like a lot of different kinds of music, but if it doesn't have any soul, I can't relate to it.

AUSTIN SUN What would you do if you couldn't play music?

VAUGHAN If I couldn't play or hear music for even a week, I'd probably check out. It's a life. I figure it's something that's going to take me past this, because it doesn't stop here. There's no reason for anybody to believe it does.

AUSTIN SUN Is religion part of your life?

VAUGHAN I'm really not sure about all of my beliefs as of yet, because every time I turn around I find out something new. I'm always in a constant battle with myself. As far as music goes, the truth to me is in what I sing—what I tell somebody with my mouth—or in what I tell with my guitar. I'm going to keep trying to get truer and truer to what I'm trying to do. I was gifted with music for a reason, and it wasn't just to get famous.

AUSTIN SUN Have you always sung and played?

VAUGHAN Not really. When I was younger, I'd try and sing some, but I didn't really work hard at it. But it's like there has always been a constant flow of reasons to play. It's probably due to something real serious that's in the air. The music that comes out of Texas has always seemed deeper. To me, anyway.

[3]

ike my brother Jimmie says, I play like
I'm breaking out of jail."
—*STEVIE RAY VAUGHAN*

BEFORE THE FLOOD

From the roadhouses of Austin comes
Stevie Ray Vaughan, riding his Stratocaster
to blues greatness on *Texas Flood*.

BY FRANK JOSEPH

PRESENCE—THE ABILITY TO MAKE DIRECT, emotional contact with a listener's heart—is that elusive intangible for which all guitarists strive and few attain. Stevie Ray Vaughan, Texas blues man, has presence to spare. His razor-edged guitar impacts emotionally on David Bowie's space-age funk opus, *Let's Dance* and simultaneously on Vaughan's debut album, *Texas Flood*, and firmly establishes him in the fertile ranks of Lone Star blues masters.

Just slightly more than a year ago Vaughan was known only in barrooms across Texas, where his band, Double Trouble—drummer Chris Layton, guitarist Johnny Winter and veteran bassist Tommy Shannon—plied their special brand of blues. From that dead-end roadhouse existence, Stevie's gut-wrenching vibrato and intense, machine-gun delivery began catching the ears of some important people. Two noted juke-joint prowlers, Rolling Stones Mick Jagger and Keith Richards, caught Double Trouble at a Dallas club and flew the band up to New York to play at a private party. The Stones expressed interest in signing Double Trouble to their RS label, though they never followed through with a contract. But when Stones roll, they make waves. Noted producer and talent-hunter Jerry Wexler arranged a move that proved to be, both literally and figuratively, a giant step for Stevie's guitar-led group.

"Jerry had heard us in an Austin club," Vaughan explains, "and he contacted the director of the 1982 Montreux Jazz Festival and got us booked there." The invitation to appear was a double honor, as Double Trouble became, on the strength of Wexler's recommendation, the first act ever to perform at Montreux without an album.

Though Stevie Ray was a bit intimidated by Montreux's heavy-weight lineup—"We weren't sure how we'd be accepted"—the searing licks that emanated from his array of classic Stratocasters won over the international audience. And any lingering doubts Vaughan may have had were alleviated by a request from David Bowie.

"As soon as we were finished," Stevie says of his introduction to rock's Man of a Thousand Faces, "someone came backstage and told us David Bowie wanted to meet us." The English art rocker and Texas blues trio headed over "to the musician's bar at the casino," Vaughan details, "where we talked for hours. We ended up playing at the bar for several nights, and Jackson Browne came in and jammed with us."

As it turned out, Bowie was preparing to record an "underlying R&B work," and with some persistence hired Stevie to play lead on

Let's Dance and in his band for his current world tour. Since the first of the year Bowie has made a point of informing the music media that "Stevie is the most exciting city blues stylist I've heard in years." Going a step further, Bowie has placed Double Trouble on the bill for his outdoor U.S. concerts, insuring the widest possible exposure for Vaughan.

Jackson Browne, whose interest wasn't quite so vested as Bowie's, offered Stevie his Down Town studio to record an album that would win Double Trouble a record deal. The LP was presented to the legendary producer John Hammond, Sr., whose greatest discoveries—Count Basie, Charlie Christian, Bob Dylan, Aretha Franklin, Bruce Springsteen—are all groundbreakers in the pantheon of American popular music. "Immensely excited" by Vaughan's "freshness," Hammond purchased the album, *Texas Flood*, and signed Double Trouble to the CBS-distributed label bearing his name. From his Manhattan office, the music industry's most respected maven remarks, "I was so delighted by Stevie's sound—it's unlike anyone else's—and he's such a marvelous improviser, never repeating exactly the same thing twice." In addition, Hammond was impressed by the band's "strong ensemble sense."

That "sense" is a result of Vaughan and company's having performed almost nightly since Double Trouble was formed in May 1979. In order to preserve the band's symbiotic intensity, *Texas Flood* (except for some of the vocals) was recorded live in the studio, without overdubbing or headphones. Vaughan's insistence on this point led to a most unusual occurrence, which underscores the trio's precision.

"In the middle of one of the tunes I broke a string and we had to stop," Vaughan recalls. "After I changed the string we picked up right where we left off—and punched back in at the same time. I don't know if this has ever been done before. The engineer sort of looked at us weird, but we got it on the first take." Stevie laughs, refusing to reveal the song's title, challenging listeners to guess for themselves.

Hammond personally took the role of executive producer for *Texas Flood*. "There was a strange balance, and we spent a lot of time remixing it," he says. It is a job he obviously relished, however. "I can't take too much credit for Stevie. He came to me, and that's almost unique in my experience. Only one other person has done that—Bruce Springsteen—and that's pretty good company."

Hammond has in his career been intimately involved with the development of such guitar giants as Eddie Lang, Charlie Christian and George Benson. Of this rather select group, he states, "They are all on the highest possible plateau, and Stevie's right up there with them. There's nothing artificial about his presence—it's honest music." Drawing an analogy between two of the celebrated guitarists and Vaughan, Hammond comments, "Charlie came in and gave Benny [*Goodman*] new life, and I think Stevie's doing the same for David Bowie. Eddie Lang was a trailblazer in the Twenties and Thirties, and Stevie's a trailblazer in the Eighties. He's the true kind of creative force that one looks for but rarely finds. He's truly original, and I automatically compare him to Robert Johnson because Stevie's got that unique passion."

Passion for the blues and the guitar's presence is a family tradition for Vaughan, whose brother Jimmie, the excellent guitarist for the Fabulous Thunderbirds, was a strong role model during their childhood in a Dallas suburb. "I wanted to play saxophone, but all I could get were a few squeaks," remembers Stevie, who first picked up a guitar in 1963. "So, my big brother was playing guitar and I figured I'd try it, too."

Loving it from the get-go, Stevie progressed from "a cardboard copy of a Roy Rogers" to his first electric model and amp, a hollow-body Gibson Messenger and a Silvertone. The Silvertone was soon supplemented by a Fender Champion 600. Vaughan remarks, "I had the right kind of amps from the beginning."

Within a year, Stevie was exposed to the classic licks of B.B., Freddie and Albert King, Albert Collins and other electric blues masters "on the records Jimmie brought home." As his interest in the guitar inflamed, Stevie began pestering his brother for lessons. "Jimmie showed me a lot of stuff," the younger Vaughan credits, "but there was a time when he warned, 'If you ask me to show you anything again, I'll kick your ass.' Well, I did and he did!"

Also at this time, Stevie heard the blistering guitar instrumental "Wham," by Lonnie Mack, whose supercharged lines and tone heavily influenced Vaughan's mature style.

"Lonnie was ahead of his time, but at the same time he was right in there with Albert Collins' 'cool sounds.' "

Sixteen years later Vaughan had the thrill of meeting his guitar hero. "Lonnie came into an Austin club where we were playing. I asked him if he would play, but Lonnie, the master of the Flying V, said he wouldn't touch anything but a Gibson [*Vaughan's arsenal was all vintage Strats*], and so he just got up and sang his ass off. Later he said he wanted to produce us."

By 1966 Vaughan was trying his first Fender guitar, a '52 Broadcaster he borrowed from his brother Jimmie. Two years later, at 14 (and now using a black '54 Les Paul TV model, again supplied by his brother), Stevie joined his first full-time band, Blackbird. Shortly after joining Blackbird, which had a strong following on the Dallas club circuit, Stevie purchased a '52 gold-top Les Paul.

Today a confirmed "Fender man," who is the proud owner of four classic Stratocasters, Vaughan says of the Gibson solid-bodies: "I never dug regular Les Pauls with that dirty sound, though I liked Jimmie's TV model because it was real clear. The '52 sounded good, too, because it had whistlers [*Gibson "soapbar" pickups*] and not humbuckers, which I'd never use." If not quite a Les Paul fan, Stevie has come to appreciate "the better Gibson hollow-bodies. I had a Barney Kessel that I got 11 years ago that I really enjoyed until 1975, when it was ripped off, and now there's my '59 dot-neck 335." Vaughan appreciates the dot-neck 335 because "it sounds and feels pretty. It has a real strong bass response, and at the same time it's real bright." Concerning the prized neck, he says, "All dot-necks are different; mine's not too thin or big around like a log. But it's wide, which is important because I have big hands, and it fits me real well."

> "Between sets I'd sneak over to the black places **to hear blues musicians.**"
> —*STEVIE RAY VAUGHAN*

In 1969 Vaughan purchased his first Stratocaster, a '63 maple-neck. He began absorbing Jimi Hendrix's epochal, blues-rooted guitar explorations, at the same time frequenting black venues to experience traditional R&B players first hand. Recalls Stevie, "Blackbird, though basically an R&B band, played all-white clubs. But between sets I'd sneak over to the black places to hear blues musicians. It got to the point where I was making my living at white clubs and having my fun at the other places." Stevie's fun was derived from seeing fine local acts like Big Boy and the Arrows and established virtuosos like B.B. and Albert King, Albert Collins, Buddy Guy, Bobby "Blue" Bland with Wayne Bennet and Howlin' Wolf with Hubert Sumlin—"the same people I'd go see now if they were still around."

Stevie is quick to cite Magic Sam, Otis Rush and his brother Jimmie as prime influences, but perhaps more than any other guitarist, Jimi Hendrix left the most indelible mark on Vaughan's playing. "I love Hendrix for so many reasons," he states with great reverence. "He was so much more than just a blues guitarist—he played damn well any kind of guitar he wanted. In fact I'm not sure if he even played the guitar—he played music."

Vaughan was not particularly pleased with the Stratocaster he bought in 1969. "It was constantly giving me trouble and driving me nuts," he says of the '63 maple-neck. So, for the remainder of his high school years, he switched "back and forth between the '52 and '54 Les Pauls, and the '52 Broadcaster," before settling on the Gibson Barney Kessel hollow-body in 1972.

Following high school Stevie relocated to Austin, a city blossoming with music opportunities. On a return gig to Dallas in 1973 with his new band, the Nightcrawlers, Vaughan arranged a trade for what would become the most important guitar he ever owned.

"I walked into this guitar store carrying my '63 Strat," he recalls, "and I saw this other Strat hanging in the window. I just had to have it—I hadn't even played it, but I knew by the way it looked it sounded great—and I asked if they wanted to trade." The "new" guitar—Stevie's prize '59 rosewood Stratocaster—became his main ax from the moment he acquired it.

Though Vaughan calls the Strat "my '59," the guitar's true age is somewhat unclear. "It was officially put out in 1962," he explains, "but the neck is stamped '59. When I got it there was a sticker under the bass pickup that read 'L.F. '59.' So I think Leo Fender put it together with spare parts and issued it in '62. But it doesn't really matter to me; all I know is that I've never found another one that sounds like it."

One spare part Stevie is especially fond of is the rosewood neck. "The neck is shaped differently from most others. It's a D-neck, but it's oddly shaped—it's real, real big, and fits my hand like a glove."

"My yellow '64 is very strange," is how Stevie describes another of his beloved Strats. "It was owned by the lead guitar player for Vanilla Fudge, who trashed it by putting four humbuckers in it. Charley Wirz [*of Charley's Guitar Shop in Dallas*] gave it to me a couple of years ago, and I had him fix it up and put one stock treble Fender pickup in it. The body rings like a bell because it's practically hollow—the middle was cut out for the humbuckers—and the only part that's solid is the edge." Vaughan used his "bell-like" Strat to record "Tell Me," from *Texas Flood*.

Stevie left the Nightcrawlers in 1973 to take the guitar chair in the Cobras, a long-established, Austin-based R&B band. Two years later, he helped form Triple Threat, with whom he played "as much R&B as I could pull off." Patterned after an R&B revue, Triple Threat featured an unusual lineup that included five lead singers, among them Stevie himself. In early 1978 the band folded, and with Triple Threat singer Lu Ann Barton he organized Double Trouble, named after his favorite Otis Rush song.

As may be discerned from *Texas Flood*, Double Trouble is decidedly not a power trio in the conventional sense. Vaughan's guitar dominates the sound. "Lots of times I'll play lead and rhythm together," he says. "I play as many different things—piano, sax and harp parts—as I can at once. Whatever I can fit, whenever I need to."

A hallmark of Stevie's playing is its broad-ranging, tasteful versatility. The glass-breaking vibrato, torrid showers of licks, driving chords and occasional feedback have managed to please both hard-core blues purists and high-energy rock fans, a circumstance obviously not lost on David Bowie.

"I don't know what kind of music you'd call it," says Stevie of Bowie's album, "but I tried to play like Albert King and it seemed to fit."

Vaughan's description is a bit too modest. While he relied more on his King-like wailing vibrato than on his arsenal of hot licks, it is very doubtful whether Albert King and his Flying V could have so seamlessly fit into Bowie's work. Like two of his heroes, Lonnie Mack and Jimi Hendrix, Vaughan has successfully integrated blues guitar in music far removed from the style's original contexts. That is what John Hammond refers to as Stevie's "freshness."

The truly killer aspects of Vaughan's playing are his fat tone and full-bodied clarity, which combined constitute one of the most formidable sounds in guitardom. Stevie Ray attributes his power to his picking technique, string setup and equipment. "Most people can't bend my strings," he states matter-of-factly. "The gauges I'm using now—.013, .016, .019, .028, .038, .056—are small for me, but if I use 'em any bigger, I tear my fingers off." Vaughan also has a habit of tearing his frets off. "The way I play, I go through a set in a year. So I put '58 Gibson Jumbo Bass frets on all my necks." To facilitate string-bending Vaughan tunes his guitar to E♭.

Stevie has over the years searched for the right combination of amplifiers and speakers. His quest will end "as soon as I get enough money to buy a Dumble. I can't say enough good things about those amps." Stevie used Jackson Browne's Mother Dumble to record *Texas Flood*. Meanwhile, Vaughan employs a Marshall Combo with two 12-inch JBLs and two Fender Vibraverbs, no. 5 and 6, with one 15-inch JBL. "My amps are backward," he laughs. "I use the Fenders for distortion and the Marshall for clarity." He adds, "The Marshall is supposed to be 200 watts, but mine's never worked right; it peaks out at 80."

Onstage Stevie uses only one Fender head, as he runs a Y cord from his guitar to the Marshall and one of the Vibraverbs, an obscure 50-watt amp which Fender marketed in the early Sixties. The other Fender serves as a speaker cabinet.

For Bowie's album, Vaughan played through a rented post-CBS Super Reverb; for the tour, he says, he "just bought two Mesa/Boogies. I don't even know what models they are—they're the small wooden ones. The reason I'm using them is they sound a lot like a Dumble. But that doesn't mean I'm not going to buy a Dumble as soon as I get the money!"

All of Vaughan's guitars have stock pickups. He occasionally employs two devices, an Ibanez Tube Screamer and Vox wah-wah pedal, to beef up his sound. "I use the Tube Screamer because of the tone knob," he says. "That way you can vary the distortion and tonal range. You can turn it on slightly to get a Guitar Slim tone, which is how I use it, or wide open so your guitar sounds like it should jump up and bite you." None of the devices were used for *Let's Dance*. The Tube Screamer did its dirty work on two *Texas Flood* cuts: the title track and, in conjunction with the wah-wah, "Testify."

Equipment aside, one of the most crucial elements of Vaughan's sound is the way he uses his fingers. "Sometimes I slide 'em, rubbing the sides of the strings," he explains. "To get a big, fat sound that punches out I pop the strings with either my second or third finger. Usually I'll hold the pick but ignore it, and get my second or third finger under the string, pull it and let go. Basically, it's what modern bass players do—it gives me a real bright, poppier tone. But now I can get that same tone with my thumb, just by laying into the string a little harder." Here Vaughan pauses to laugh at himself. "But like my brother Jimmie says, I play like I'm breaking out of jail anyway."

REPRINTED FROM *GUITAR WORLD*, FEBRUARY 2004

[4]

"Eventually addiction set in, and
we knew we had to stop."
—*TOMMY SHANNON*

GUITAR HURRICANE

Double Trouble's Tommy Shannon and Chris Layton
deliver a dramatic, eyewitness account
of Stevie Ray Vaughan's brilliant performances on
Texas Flood and *Couldn't Stand the Weather*.

BY ANDY ALEDORT

LONG BEFORE BASSIST Tommy Shannon cut records with Stevie Ray Vaughan, he knew the guitarist as an outsider on the Austin blues scene—a punk kid whose concept of the blues was too radical for the local purists.

"Everyone on the scene treated Stevie cruel, for years," says Shannon. "People don't talk about it much, but it's true. When I first saw him, he was like a little pigeon-toed kid. He was looked at like a pest, and at the time he had a personality that was kind of awkward. Some of the musicians he respected treated him so cruelly."

"The great thing was that he could play fucking better than any of them," notes drummer Chris Layton, Shannon's partner in Double Trouble, the duo that backed Stevie famously live and on record. "It's true."

"The very last thing anyone expected out of Stevie back then," adds Shannon, "was that he would become a big success."

But Stevie Ray Vaughan became more than a success—he became a blues trailblazer, and an inspiration to a new generation of guitarists that includes Kirk Hammett and John Mayer. He did so precisely because he refused to be constrained by tradition. The album that changed everything—for Stevie *and* for electric blues—was *Texas Flood*, Stevie Ray Vaughan and Double Trouble's incendiary debut. Recorded as a demo in just two days, *Texas Flood* became a smash hit. With it, Stevie Ray Vaughan gave notice to all—including his detractors—that the blues was still an evolving and influential musical force. In two decades' time, the album's legacy—and that of the band that made it—has continued to strengthen with each passing year.

In the opinion of many SRV fans, *Texas Flood* captured Stevie Ray Vaughan at the height of his powers. It was the first record by which most people became acquainted with the mysterious new guitar virtuoso, who was then burning up the airwaves as the featured guitarist on David Bowie's hit single "Let's Dance." From the first notes of *Texas Flood*'s high-velocity opener, "Love Struck Baby," the album sounds like a live gig—which is appropriate, since all the tracks were cut live, most of them in one day. The intensity of Stevie's playing, combined with the air-tight interaction of Shannon and Layton, makes *Texas Flood* a brilliant example of Texas blues rock at its finest. Stevie and Double Trouble sound lean, mean and hungry, and they were—they had no record deal at the time of the recording and were desperately in search of one.

"When I think of *Texas Flood* and its follow-up, *Couldn't Stand the Weather*," says Shannon, "I think of exactly what Stevie said: 'We had our whole lives to make *Texas Flood*, but we had to start from scratch with *Couldn't Stand the Weather*.' *Texas Flood* was banged out in two days with no time to second-guess at all. *Couldn't Stand the Weather* was our first 'real' record with a real budget. But by then, so many things had changed for us, in every way."

The story of Stevie's "overnight" success is well known, but here it is in a nutshell: Atlantic Records honcho Jerry Wexler caught Stevie Ray and Double Trouble at the Continental Club in Austin, Texas, and was so impressed that he helped book the band at the Montreux Jazz Festival. (They remain the only unsigned act ever to play this prestigious event.) The European audience booed SRV's brand of high-volume blues, but two people in attendance, Jackson Browne and David Bowie, were knocked out. Browne offered the band free studio time, and Bowie invited Stevie to appear on his next studio album, *Let's Dance*, and its subsequent tour.

Stevie, Chris and Tommy entered Jackson's Down Town studio in L.A. on Thanksgiving weekend of 1982, and emerged two days later with the tapes that would become *Texas Flood*. While they were in town, Bowie called and arranged for Stevie to come onboard. While Stevie was rehearsing with Bowie, legendary record producer John Hammond Sr. used the Down Town recordings to secure a deal with Epic Records, which packaged the demos as *Texas Flood*. Released in June 1983, *Texas Flood* blasted off the shelves, and Stevie Ray Vaughan was quickly hailed as a phenomenal new guitar hero.

"I think *Texas Flood* is one of the best records we ever made," says Shannon. "It's so basic—there's nothing fancy going on—which is why it sounds so powerful, too."

Although a mere six months passed between the release of *Texas Flood* and the start of the recording sessions for the band's next effort, *Couldn't Stand the Weather*, a great deal changed for the band, professionally and personally, in that short period. *Couldn't Stand the Weather* represented the first time the band had a recording budget, but with it came record company pressures that had been absent from the sessions for the previous album. In addition, as the pace of the band members' careers increased, so did the level of partying and drug use. Still, *Couldn't Stand the Weather* reveals the blossoming of SRV as a guitarist, singer and songwriter; it showcases an artist and a band still on the rise, spreading its wings and flying higher and higher.

By 1986, however, Stevie Ray Vaughan and Double Trouble were flying a little too high. Drug intake landed Stevie in rehab, but he emerged with newfound enthusiasm that was well demonstrated on the band's next studio release, 1989's *In Step*, a masterpiece that yielded the Number One hit "Crossfire," a song cowritten by Layton and Shannon. Then, on August 27, 1990, Stevie's life ended suddenly and tragically in a helicopter crash following a show at Alpine Valley, Wisconsin.

In the 14 years since Stevie's passing, Shannon and Layton have kept Double Trouble alive through a variety of recording dates and live gigs with artists such as the Arc Angels, Storyville, Buddy Guy, Buddy Miles, Susan Tedeschi and Kenny Wayne Shepherd. Moreover, they remain in great demand, as was proven when John Mayer, the pop music wünderkind and a major SRV fanatic, tapped the duo for his appearance on *Austin City Limits*, the live music television show produced in Shannon and Layton's hometown. (The program with Mayer and Double Trouble aired nationally on November 15, 2003.) The show also featured legendary blues guitarist Buddy Guy, and discussions are taking place for Mayer, Guy and Double Trouble to play some live shows together.

In addition, both men have engaged in a variety of solo projects. This past fall, Shannon reunited Krackerjack, the band he formed in 1970 with Uncle John Turner following their split from Johnny Winter. Original members of the group include Mike Kindred—keyboardist and the co-composer of the *Couldn't Stand the Weather* hit "Cold Shot"—singer Bruce Bowland and guitarist John Stahely.

Layton, for his part, recently hooked up with Gordie Johnson, guitarist for the Canadian band Big Sugar, and along with bassist Ben Richardson formed a band called Grady. In addition, Double Trouble recently made an as-yet-unreleased record with a young guitarist from Oklahoma named Shane Henry.

> "We never made a record more honest than *Texas Flood*."
> —CHRIS LAYTON

Recently, Chris, Tommy and I sat down in South Austin to talk about the making of *Texas Flood* and *Couldn't Stand the Weather*, and how these two milestone recordings changed their lives and the course of electric blues.

GUITAR WORLD What are some of the first things that come to mind when you think about *Texas Flood*?

TOMMY SHANNON I always think of this one particular instance: a few weeks after the album was released, we went to Hollywood to play the Palace, a club we'd played before to mediocre crowds. This time, there was a line going all the way down the street and around the block! That's when we first realized the album was selling like crazy.

CHRIS LAYTON We did a six-week tour right after *Texas Flood* came out, and every show was sold out—people out the door, around the block.

SHANNON I think part of that is due to the guitar tone on that record; *Texas Flood* has the best tone Stevie ever got on any of our records. Some of that had to do with the Dumble amps he had discovered at the time.

LAYTON Plus, we never made a record more *honest* than *Texas Flood*. It's like we walked out there naked and said, here we are. Because we were just making music; we weren't making a record for a record company to release.

So I think those two things really set the record in a class by itself: like Tommy said, the guitar tone is amazing; and the performance is pure, honest and bare. Plus, it's a great *band* record.

SHANNON It is. We were super-tight. What you hear is a kick-ass band, all contributing to the spirit and the sound together.

LAYTON It was an exciting time because of the innocence. Although we were already successful musically, we were still thinking, How long will I be fighting to keep the electricity and the gas on? Once Epic got interested in the band, that's when it became clear that all those events—going to Switzerland to play Montreux, meeting Jackson Browne and David Bowie—represented the pieces of our careers falling into place, and that's when it became real exciting. We realized that we *could* get a tour bus, go play some good gigs, get some good food backstage—all of the things that represent being a successful band on the road. Later on, you take all of these things for granted, but back then it was something we could only dream about.

GW Did the band see Jackson Browne's offer as a great opportunity to get a record deal?

LAYTON No, not at all. The great opportunity was that we didn't have a pot to piss in and we were going to get to record for free, not that it was our big break.

GW How much planning went into choosing the songs you recorded?

SHANNON Making that record, we just stuck to what we were passionate about. There was no planning to it whatsoever. That great thing is that people caught onto it and loved what we did. There was no big push from the record company—they didn't get behind us with ad money or tour support. It was all word of mouth that sold *Texas Flood*.

GW *Texas Flood* also benefited from the release a few months earlier of David Bowie's *Let's Dance*, the title track of which featured great Albert King–inspired solos from Stevie, who was then unknown.

LAYTON Using Stevie was a stroke of genius on Bowie's part. His guitar playing really jumped through that track, and "China Girl," too. *Let's Dance* was the advertising and the advance for *Texas Flood*. It really stoked people's interest and curiosity about Stevie.

GW Before the offer to record at Jackson Browne's studio came in, you had a few other prospects. For one, Mick Jagger had considered signing Stevie to a record deal.

LAYTON There had been some rumblings. John Hammond's original plan was to sign us to a label called HME, but that fell by the wayside. And we went to a party at Danceteria in New York specifically to play for Mick Jagger, but nothing came of it. We were still playing shitty gigs, making no money. Everything was wide open. The only thing intriguing in our lives was that we had gone to Montreux, and as exciting as it was, it seemed like a long way to go for very little money. There was no way to know that it would be the most important gig of our lives.

GW Was Stevie already onboard with Bowie when you went into Down Town?

LAYTON Bowie had expressed interest in hiring Stevie the very first night he met him. Bowie ended up calling the Oakland Garden apartments where we were staying while we were still recording at Down Town. We had set up some gigs on the West Coast, and we discovered that it was cheaper to get an apartment and drive to the gigs around the L.A./Ventura area every night. We had *no* money, so we had to play gigs to be able to afford to live. Two of the days were set aside to record.

The truth is that, other than the offer from Jackson, we were back to square one after Montreux, with no real prospects at all. But Bowie called at 3 A.M.: "Hello, is Stevie Vaughan there?" and I thought, Who the hell is calling us at 3 A.M.? So after waiting so long for something to happen, there was an interesting tempo to how fast the pieces fell together.

GW Did you fly all of your gear out to L.A. for the recording sessions?

LAYTON Fly? We drove 1,500 miles from Austin, all of us and our gear crammed in a high-cube van, which was a converted milk truck, dubbed Sky King. It was aptly named because we got airborne on the trip when I hit an entrance ramp a little too fast, going west on I-20. We had a bed in there that we took turns sleeping on. It was suspended on a track.

SHANNON Every time you hit the brakes, the bed would go flying forward. We had just enough money for gas to get to our gigs in California.

GW What happened when you arrived at Jackson's Studio?

LAYTON Jackson's engineer, Greg Ladanyi, was there at Jackson's request to take care of us, but unbeknownst to us at the time, he was going though some personal issues. I don't think he really wanted to be there. We'd brought in [*producer/engineer*] Richard Mullen, and the first thing that happened was that we almost came to blows! We said, "Hey, we brought our own engineer," and the reaction was, "Jackson sent me here to set this up for you guys, and I'm taking care of the studio."

SHANNON That was within the first minute of being there, and suddenly it didn't seem like such a good idea after all.

LAYTON [*laughs*] We didn't want a big hassle; we just wanted to put some songs on tape. We made a few calls, and Greg finally said, "I don't want to be here anyway," and left. We'd spent about half a day going through this political stuff, so it was already late when we tried to get down to the business of recording. There was no real format or set list, and we sure didn't approach it like we were making a record.

SHANNON I think we only got two songs that first day. By the time we'd gone through all of that, and then got Richard behind the board and got sounds, that's all we had time for. We came back the next day and ran through everything.

GW How did you set up in the studio?

LAYTON The studio was a big warehouse, about 20,000 square feet, and we set up in the middle like a gig, in close proximity to each other, but facing each other in a little triangle. Stevie and Tommy were only about six or seven feet away from me. We used no iso [*isolation*] booths, no go-bos [*partitions*], nothing like that. It was wild; we just set up and played, with bleed [*microphone leakage between the instruments*] all over the place.

GW Did Stevie say he wanted to focus on his original tunes, like "Love Struck Baby" and "Pride and Joy"?

LAYTON No. All the songs were equally important to Stevie. We had a big bag of songs to draw from, so we just picked tunes off the tops of our heads, recorded them and then said, "Hey, how'd that sound?"

Mullen would say, "Sounds pretty good." And we'd move on from there. Stevie became more interested in his originals by the time of *Couldn't Stand the Weather*.

SHANNON I remember that we did "Pride and Joy," "Texas Flood" and "Testify" the second day. We took a run at "Texas Flood" the first day, but the second day was better. When we did "Testify," Stevie broke a string halfway through. So we cued up the spot and punched in the whole band. I defy anyone to hear that punch-in.

LAYTON I think we ended up using two songs from the first day and eight songs from the second day, but that was just how it turned out.

GW Did Stevie do any of the vocals in L.A.?

SHANNON No, he did all the vocals back in Austin at Riverside Sound.

GW Are there any complete alternate takes of any of the songs on *Texas Flood* still in the can?

LAYTON That's a good question. I can't honestly say. I would doubt it, because of the time constraint.

GW Did Stevie bring any specific amps or guitars to the sessions?

SHANNON That's when he discovered Dumble amps. He used a Dumble that belonged to Jackson dubbed Mother Dumble, and it had mud all over the back of it. He didn't get his own Dumbles till later.

LAYTON He used some Fender amps, too, I think. Stevie tried the Dumble and said, "That sounds *great*. Let's play." I pulled the drums out of the truck, set them up, never even tuned 'em, and we began recording.

GW It sounds like the things that usually happen when you make a record—hit the drums, go listen, play some guitar, go listen, et cetera—never happened because there was no time.

LAYTON That's right. It was the anti-record! [*laughs*] We didn't do any of that, and this record proves that all of that stuff doesn't really matter. The only reason it's a record is because it was recorded.

SHANNON I have always felt that there's a strong correlation between *Texas Flood* and the first record I made with Johnny Winter, *The Progressive Blues Experiment*. Both were done for virtually no money, and both are just raw blues played by a trio. *Progressive Blues* was recorded at a club in Austin called the Vulcan Gas Company, in the daytime, with no one there, on a little two-track reel-to-reel. We blasted through it like it was a gig, with no isolation between the instruments, and it turned out to be, in my opinion, a great record. Both of these records were identical in that respect. *Progressive Blues* is my favorite Johnny record, and *Texas Flood* is my favorite Stevie record, along with *In Step*.

GW What happened immediately after recording *Texas Flood*? Did Stevie feel really excited about the tapes?

LAYTON No, I can't remember him expressing that at all. It was like a day at the office; we cared, but it wasn't that big a deal. Afterward, we did a few more West Coast dates and went back home. Then Stevie started recording with Bowie in January of '83, and there were discussions that we would open for Bowie on the tour. So Stevie began rehearsing for the tour, and Tommy and I were just sitting here in Austin, wondering what would happen. At that point, the *Texas Flood* tapes were taken to somewhere in South Austin and left in someone's garage.

One day, we were sitting with Cutter [*Brandenburg, Stevie's close friend and Double Trouble's road manager*] and we said, "Goddamn, we need to do something with those tapes!" Necessity is the mother of invention, and the one thing that made the most sense for Stevie, Tommy and myself was to get those recordings exposed. Even though Stevie was looking at a heavy commitment to Bowie, interest in the tapes would have reminded him of where his heart lay—of what it was he really always wanted, which was to have his own band. Buried in a garage, the tapes could have been forgotten.

So Tommy, Cutter and I called Chesley Millikin, our manager, to talk about the tapes, and he said [*in a gruff voice*], "Don't bother me! Stevie's busy with David Bowie!" We asked him to take the tapes to John Hammond or somebody and see if we could get a deal. He said, "Well, that's not a bad idea." He called John, and John took the tapes to Greg Geller at CBS and said, "You've got to sign this guy!"

Signing Stevie made sense, because Stevie was on Bowie's next record, which they fig- ured would blow up huge, and he was going to tour all over the world with him. There was our marketing, right there. It was the perfect time to sign him, even for a modest advance and investment.

"Expecting Stevie to get back in a milk truck **after two years with Bowie** seemed ridiculous."
—*CHRIS LAYTON*

So those things started to come together while Stevie was rehearsing with Bowie, and suddenly he had to choose between touring with Bowie or doing what he always wanted to do, which was to tour with his own band. He was thinking, Here's my guys, waiting in the wings, and those tapes are going to be released as a record, and this could be the beginning of the career of Stevie Ray Vaughan and Double Trouble. If the tapes hadn't been dug up right when they were, everything else may never have happened.

Stevie keep us on salary while he rehearsed with Bowie, which was funny because we never had been on salary before! Asking management to keep us on salary while Stevie toured with Bowie for 18 months, two years, made us wonder, Once Stevie's done touring with Bowie, is everything going to be just like it was before? Expecting Stevie to get back in a milk truck after two years with Bowie seemed ridiculous, so we thought that we'd better up the ante and try for salvation.

GW And as Stevie's relationship with Bowie fell apart, the tapes in the garage ended up being just that.

LAYTON Exactly. The irony was that, at one moment, the tapes weren't important at all; the next moment, they represented *everything*, which they should have from the beginning. It all changed in 24 hours when Stevie opted out of the Bowie tour. As a result, part of the setup for the release of *Texas Flood* became, "Who is this nobody guitar player from Texas that just walked out on David Bowie?" That was bigger news than if he'd done the tour.

GW Any favorite tracks on *Texas Flood*?

LAYTON I like "Mary Had a Little Lamb" because it's so tight. It sounds really funny to say, but the way we all hit that one note together after Stevie says "Tiskit" always sounded cool to me. And the guitar tone on the opening of "Pride and Joy" is as good as, if not better than, anything I've ever heard, just in terms of pure tone. Some of that speaks to the innocence and the magic of those days. That's something you don't even realize till much later.

SHANNON I really like "Texas Flood" because I'd never heard anyone play a slow blues like that. It's more intense than a traditional blues. It was as if we crossed over into something new, with a different attitude. That attitude led us to do "Voodoo Chile" on the next record, and we used that same approach when we played some of the straight blues songs, too.

GW How did the *Texas Flood* experience compare with the recording of *Couldn't Stand the Weather*?

SHANNON You couldn't find two more different records in terms of the recording process. One wasn't even meant to be a record, and the other one was all about being a *record*, ceremoniously.

LAYTON In January of '84, Epic flew us to New York to record at the Power Station, which was the hottest studio, and we stayed in nice hotels for six weeks. There was intellectualizing going on: A&R and the marketing people wanted to come in for a listening party midstream and evaluate the recording. They had all kinds of ideas about how to make a "great" record, and Stevie didn't want the record company people in the studio *at all*. Stevie said to them, "You think we did pretty good on the first one, don't you?" And they said, "Oh, it's wonderful." So he said, "Then we don't need your help on the second one."

"By the time we get to recording *Couldn't Stand the Weather*, the drug intake had increased dramatically."
—*TOMMY SHANNON*

Stevie didn't want any of the music to get out of the studio till we were done, but a guy from the record company came in one night after we were gone and took some tracks out. Stevie called him up and ripped him a new asshole: "Don't you *ever* fuckin' come in and take my music. I don't give a fuck if you're with the record company!" He was furious: "Don't you ever steal my music from me again!"

GW Did this kind of pressure interfere with working on the record?

LAYTON Not really. There was none of that "sophomore jinx" stuff. But I did begin to think about all the money that was being spent for limousines and expensive hotel bills. I could hear Chesley saying, "We've already spent $80,000 on this record!" and we were just about done with the basics. Things weren't so innocent anymore.

SHANNON By the time we got to recording *Couldn't Stand the Weather*, the drug intake had increased dramatically. We were becoming successful, so dealers were not hard to find; they found us.

LAYTON We were high on how cool it was to be recording in New York with the record company's blessing. But we were real high, too. There were two distinctly different highs going on.

GW So as the quality of the gigs and the recording sessions improved, so did the quality of the drugs?

SHANNON That's true. At that time, the negative effects of the drugs hadn't taken over yet. We were feeling great, and the drug intake was just a part of everything else. But eventually addiction set in, and we knew we had to stop.

GW Were you trying to be discreet about the drug use?

LAYTON We had to sneak around, because John Hammond was coming into the studio every day, and we tried to hide it from him. But he knew what we were up to.

SHANNON I mean, why else would a whole group of guys go crouching down behind a piano together? [*laughs*] We couldn't have been more obvious, really.

LAYTON Hammond's way of dealing with this was to tell us this story about working with [*legendary jazz drummer*] Gene Krupa. He said he thought Krupa was an incredible drummer, but not when he got high; ever since then, he didn't allow drug use on his sessions. So we got the message, even though all we did was try to hide it from him a little better.

GW For this recording, did you spent a day or two getting the sounds together?

LAYTON Not that long. Right when we started, Richard asked us to play something so he could get sounds, so I did that drum roll on the floor tom at the beginning of "Tin Pan Alley" and Stevie and Tommy just fell in. When we were done John Hammond hit the talkback mic and said, "You'll never get it better than that!" He was right; it turned out to be the track we kept. I said, "Y'all recorded that?"

GW Was there any specific preparation for the second record?

SHANNON We rehearsed in Austin before we went to New York, and Stevie worked a long time on the original songs, in particular the title track. Stevie wasn't a fluent songwriter; he'd spend a lot of time on a song, rewriting parts, and he admitted that it could be laborious. I came up with the funky guitar/bass unison lick on the title song's intro, but it was phrased differently; I had the first note falling on "two" instead of "one"—it was more like a horn line—and Stevie suggested changing that first note to the "one."

LAYTON The third time that lick is played, we wait two extra beats before we come back in, and that was something we'd never done in rehearsal. We were cutting the track, and when we reached that point, Stevie put his finger up to his lips—like "Shhh!"—and then cued us to come back in. When it came time to recreate it, we had to figure out how long that pause was.

SHANNON Actually, Jimmie [*Vaughan, Stevie's brother who plays on the track*] had mentioned to Stevie that he should try something like that, and it worked out great.

GW How did the band go about recording each track?

LAYTON We'd normally cut a tune three or four times, listen to it and then go on from there. If we didn't get a tune in a few takes, we'd try another tune. We knew that the song wouldn't get better from playing it nine or 10 times.

GW What's the story behind "Cold Shot"?

SHANNON "Cold Shot" was written by WC Clark and Mike Kindred.

Kindred played with Stevie in '72 in Krackerjack, and WC played with Stevie in Triple Threat, the band that predated Double Trouble.

LAYTON I didn't even know that Stevie was interested in cutting "Cold Shot" for the record until the very night we recorded it. And he didn't sing it at all when we cut it, so I still didn't really know what the arrangement was. That was the first time we'd ever played the song from beginning to end.

Drummers have always asked me how I got that super-laid-back, in-the-pocket feel on "Cold Shot," and the truth was I'd been awake for about 20 hours, and then fell asleep. Stevie woke me up at 4 A.M. and said, "Whipper, come in and do 'Cold Shot'! " and I said, "Oh, let's go back to the hotel, man. I'm asleep!" I got behind the drums and we cut it in one take. I remember thinking, Would this have been better if I was really rested and knew the arrangement? But you can't really answer that question because it is what it is.

GW How did Fran Christina [*drummer for the Fabulous Thunderbirds, Jimmie Vaughan's group*] come to play drums on Stevie's "Stang's Swang"?

LAYTON They all showed up in the studio because Jimmie was playing on the title track and "The Things (That) I Used to Do," and they hung out for two days. When it came time to do "Stang's Swang," I think I was unconscious on the couch [*laughs*], so Stevie said, "Fran, get over here!"

GW There were a handful of songs cut during the *Couldn't Stand the Weather* sessions that came out later: "Little Wing," "Empty Arms," "Wham" and "Close to You," which were released on the posthumous *The Sky Is Crying*; and "Come On (Pt. III)," "Hideaway," "Look At Little Sister" and "Give Me Back My Wig," which were included on the reissued version of *Couldn't Stand the Weather*.

LAYTON "Little Sister" is the song that the record company swiped out of the studio, so it's interesting that Stevie ended up not including that one on the final record. "Little Wing," "Wham" and "Close to You" were all songs we'd been playing in our live set, so it made sense to try recording them.

GW Did Stevie express his feelings about *Couldn't Stand the Weather* after you were done?

LAYTON We really didn't have time to think about it. We went right back out on the road. I never heard him say a word about it. But the record company loved it, and we went into production for two videos, "Couldn't Stand the Weather" and "Cold Shot," simultaneously, with two different directors. We were running from a scene in one video to a scene in the other video.

SHANNON The record was a success, so we were excited. New things were happening every day.

GW Do you have any favorite tracks from this record?

SHANNON "Voodoo Chile," because Stevie's playing is great and because it represented his transformation from blues into what lay ahead in the future. I really had to talk Stevie into doing that track, because he was afraid of what the "blues purists" might have to say about it. I said, "Hey, there's nothing wrong with stepping over the line." We'd started to play it live. The first time was at the old Antone's in Austin.

LAYTON We were all on the same page about that. When I first came into the band, Lou Ann Barton was still the singer, and there was a heavy, heavy blues-purist clique mentality. I wasn't from that clique, so I was looked at a little funny for a while. Playing Freddie King and Albert King was okay, but Hendrix? No way. At parties, I'd hear people saying, "What the fuck is Stevie doing playing that

Hendrix shit," as hard as that may be to believe. And I'd say, "Hey, I love it."

SHANNON It was okay for Stevie to play "Voodoo Chile"—except to the blues Nazi fundamentalists. [*laughs*] Like Stevie, I really thought it was okay to stretch the concept of the blues into something new and different, that you didn't have to play that laid-back, *predictable* boring blues that I was so fucking sick of I wanted to shoot anyone that played like that! With the exception of a really good blues band like the Fabulous Thunderbirds, there were so many bands I wanted to kill. There is nothing worse than bad blues.

LAYTON Isn't that weird? How Muddy Waters is the best shit you've ever heard, and a bar band trying to play blues is the worst shit you've ever heard?

SHANNON It pisses me off. There are so many blues purists who think the music has to be played one way and that's it. Back in the early days, there were a lot of people in town with that mentality, and Stevie wanted their respect. He was inside that circle, and he was afraid that if he stepped through it, he'd really get criticized. And he did, by the blues Nazis.

GW Tommy, you told me that when you first met Stevie in 1970 at the Fog in Dallas, he was so reverential of the older players, and they treated him really badly.

SHANNON Oh, that's true. And he was so much better than any of them. They looked at him like a little punk: "Get outta here!" Uncle John [*Turner*] and I were the only ones that would talk to him. I told him when he was a teenager, "Stevie, you are already better than all of these guys."

LAYTON Stevie had this alter ego he'd slip into for fun called "Brady," which was sort of like a dumb hick. One guy in particular used to say, "Brady, you're like someone's limping uncle."

GW Did Stevie ever give you the sense that he knew how good he was?

LAYTON In all the years I knew Stevie, there was only one occasion where I heard him acknowledge his talent as a guitar player. He and I had gone to Buddy Guy's club in Chicago, and someone had shot a video of Stevie and Buddy jamming together. After we played, we took the tape back to the hotel and Stevie popped it in the VCR. The camera was only about six feet from the stage, and there was a part where Stevie had the guitar up on his shoulder, like a violin, playing with one hand, and it was just amazing. It was like a different kind of Hendrix—Stevie Ray Hendrix. So Stevie was watching this, and he looked over at me, paused and said, "I'm good." [*laughs*] I thought that was so cool. He was so self-effacing; he never said things like that.

SHANNON I don't think Stevie ever knew how incredible he really was. He needed the encouragement to help him pursue the things that were in his heart.

LAYTON After Lou Ann left Double Trouble, the bass player was Jack Newhouse, who Tommy replaced. Jack didn't like to play anything but blues, and he didn't like playing loud.

SHANNON It didn't seem like he wanted to play, period. [*laughs*]

LAYTON When we got Tommy, all the blues purists in the band were gone, so we could play whatever we wanted. Stevie could have, of course, played whatever he wanted from the beginning, but he felt pressure from the blues community not to stray. With the three of us, we were all gunning for the same thing.

GW But embracing "heavier" music didn't happen until *Couldn't Stand the Weather*.

LAYTON That's right, and that's because it had to do with the growing encouragement. *Texas Flood* was doing well and the tours were going great, so we were inspired to take it a step further. And, truthfully, the band was headed where it was headed anyway.

SHANNON "Voodoo Chile" was one of our favorite songs, and Stevie was one of the only guitar players I ever heard beside Hendrix that could play the shit out of it. That song was responsible for bridging the gap between blues and a totally new kind of music. Young kids would hear our version of "Voodoo Chile" and dig it, and then hear our other "bluesier" songs played just as intensely, and they'd see the connection. For us, it was like we were breaking out of jail. "Voodoo Chile" turned out to be our point of departure into the future. So many musicians want to stay in "the box," but we couldn't wait to get out of it.

GW The fact is, Stevie's success came about precisely because he ventured into uncharted territory.

SHANNON That's absolutely true. The thing is that we never got away from playing blues; we got away from traditional blues. We found a new way to play blues that was all about the power of the three-piece band.

GW Did Stevie ever say if he felt he had been vindicated?

LAYTON Honestly, Stevie and I were talking about that the very last night of his life, right before he got on the helicopter. He was talking about *Family Style*, the record he'd just finished making with his brother, Jimmie, and he said, "I'm *ready*, man. I am really excited about making our next record." He said, "I needed to make that record with my brother, and we'll play a bunch of shows, but I can't wait to get to *our* next record. I have some ideas, and it's gonna be wild. We're gonna bust it wide open."

Stevie always had respect for the blues tradition and the music, but he never lost the idea that he had something to say within that context. He wanted to pay respect to the tradition, but do so while expressing his own creativity. *In Step* was really the fledgling project where he put some twists on the tradition. But he was looking forward to our next record, to really taking things to a whole new place.

REPRINTED FROM *GUITAR WORLD*, SEPTEMBER 1988

[5]

"I'm discovering that it's really
a wonderful world out there;
I just have to open
my eyes to it."
—*STEVIE RAY VAUGHAN*

RESURRECTION

Stevie Ray Vaughan walks away from drugs
and alcohol and is reborn in the blues.

BY BILL MILKOWSKI

SRV

TEVIE RAY VAUGHAN strides into the room, cutting a sharp figure with his signature snakeskin boots, gray *Late Night with David Letterman* T-shirt and cool black denim jacket, the back of which is emblazoned with the face of Dr. Martin Luther King, Jr. And though time hasn't altered his taste in clothes much—five years ago, his look was similarly Texas-bohemian—there's a new air about the man, a palpably new vibe.

Gone are the bleary eyes and the tell-tale stagger. Gone is the booze-and-coke haze that hung over his eyes, his band and his crew like a heavy shroud. A new, positive spirit permeates the entire entourage, from Stevie Ray right down to the roadies, soundmen and lighting crew. They've all come clean.

Two years ago, Vaughan would in all likelihood have waved a bottle of Old Crown whiskey in my face as he answered questions. At our first meeting, Stevie Ray seemed shy, inarticulate, guarded... maybe even a little frightened. He seldom volunteered more than one or two-word answers and rarely offered eye contact. But on this bright day in Orlando, Florida, a few hours before his show at the Bob Carr Performing Arts Centre, Stevie Ray Vaughan is a different man. He speaks with urgency and conviction and when he makes a point, he stares me down with an intense gaze, as if to make sure I absolutely catch his drift.

The new SRV is focused, physically together and spiritually anchored. He's learned about things like humanity, commitment and responsibility. He's got the proverbial new lease on life and is glad to be sharing the lessons he learned on the road back to sobriety. In concert nowadays, as he performs the anthemic ballad "Life without You" (a soulful, "Dock of the Bay"–type set-closer), he cautions his young audiences against getting caught up in bad habits and making the kind of mistakes he did.

On the 1986 *Live Alive* album, he used this same song to lecture about the evils of apartheid in South Africa. Now, after having experienced the humiliation of falling drunkenly from a concert stage, succumbing to a total physical collapse and finally entering a Georgia treatment facility in October 1986, he has transformed "Life without You" into an anthem against the evils of drugs and alcohol.

In the fervor of his rap, Vaughan takes on the aura of an evangelist preacher working a crowd. But this is no hollow pitch; Stevie Ray means every word he says, from the bottom of his heart—from the bottom of his pain. He had, in fact, hit rock-bottom and is now rededicating his life to his music and his friends and to appreciating each new day as it comes. Every day that passes without a drink or a snort is another victory for Stevie Ray Vaughan. So far, he's winning big.

"I can honestly say that I'm really glad to be alive today," he begins with that dead-serious gaze. "Because left to my own devices, I would've slowly killed myself."

He takes a sip of coffee and continues contemplatively: "I'm just doing the best I can now to keep this going...trying to grow up and remain young at the same time. I got a lot of paradoxes in my life. I guess I'm a real confused person. But there are some focused parts to my life now and I'm slowly trying to put all the pieces back together."

"Left to my own devices, I would've slowly killed myself."
—STEVIE RAY VAUGHAN

One important part of his therapy is hard work. For the past 18 months, Stevie Ray has been touring relentlessly. Backed by Double Trouble (drummer Chris Layton, bassist Tommy Shannon and keyboardist Reese Wynans), he opened the first leg of Robert Plant's North American tour before flying to Europe to headline summer blues festivals in Italy, Germany, Belgium and Holland. He's been so booked solid with one-nighters that he probably won't get into a studio to begin working on his next album until August—perhaps not even until September.

Meanwhile, touring is good for him. And now that he's a picture of physical fitness (he and the crew now spend free time on the road working out with weights and playing hoops—instead of imbibing), he's performing with a vitality that just wasn't there before.

"It had gotten to the point where—you know, you can't give somebody a dollar if you ain't got one. You can try all you want, but if you're out of gas, you just cannot give anymore. This was around the time we were mixing the *Live Alive* album. It was a real crazy period for all of us—for a long time we had a schedule that was just completely out of hand. And the only reason we put up with it was because, partly from the situation we were in and partly from doing too much coke, we thought we were super-human. I mean, the whole deal is that, when you walk onstage, you're up there bigger than life. People idolize you. And if you let that go to your head, you're in trouble. You have to keep those things in perspective, but that's hard to do when you're high on cocaine and drinking all the time."

Stevie Ray sighs. "We began to see that this schedule was taking its toll. During that period we were touring and making a record. My trick was not to sleep at all. I would stay in the studio all night long, doing mixes of the live stuff and choosing tunes. I'd leave the studio about noon, go to the hotel to grab a shower, go to the sound check and play the gig. Then I'd come back to the studio, stay there all night doing mixes, come back to the hotel the next noon, grab a shower, go to the sound check and play the gig. Then I'd come back to the studio. And then the whole thing would start all over again."

He shakes his head in disbelief. "For two straight weeks I did that. We had spread ourselves way too thin, tried to put our fingers in too many parts of the pie at the same time. It was taking its toll and the only way we could see to deal with that was, 'Oh, you're too tired? Well, here, snort some of this.'

"And between the coke and the alcohol, it had gotten to the point where I no longer had any idea what it would take to get drunk. I passed the stage where I could drink whatever I wanted to and be able to hold my liquor, so to speak. One day I could drink a quart and then the next day all I'd have to do was drink one sip to get completely smashed."

He doesn't remember exactly how much he drank the night he fell off the stage in London. Two, maybe three drinks. Maybe a quart. But it was painfully obvious at that point that something had gone dreadfully haywire with the reigning star of the rock and blues scene. John Hammond's promising protégé was drowning in a morass of self-destruction.

"I had envisioned myself just **staying high for the rest of my life.**"
—*STEVIE RAY VAUGHAN*

"I would wake up and guzzle something, just to get rid of the pain I was feeling. Whiskey, beer, vodka, whatever was handy. It got to the point where if I'd try to say 'hi' to somebody, I would just fall apart, crying and everything. It was like...solid doom. There really was nowhere to go but up. I'd been trying to pull myself up by my bootstraps, so to speak, but they were broken, you know?"

He exacerbated his mental, physical and spiritual decline with the help of some unfortunate "recreational" activities, the most effective of which involved pouring cocaine into his drinks to prolong the buzz. "I tore up my stomach real bad by doing that. I didn't realize that the cocaine would crystallize in my stomach and make cuts inside there. Finally, I had a breakdown. I mean, everything fell apart. I surrendered to the fact that I didn't know how to go without the stuff. I had envisioned myself just staying high for the rest of my life, you know? But I had to give up to win, because I was in a losing battle."

In September of 1986, he entered a clinic in London, under the care and supervision of Dr. Victor Bloom. "He filled me in on the disease of alcoholism and made me realize that this thing had been going on for a long time with me, long before I ever started playing professionally. Fact is, I had been drinking since 1960—when I was six years old. That's when I first started stealing Daddy's drinks. When my parents were gone, I'd find the bottle and make myself one. I thought it was cool...thought the kids down the street would think it was cool. That's where it began and I had been depending on it ever since."

Stevie Ray readily admits that just prior to his breakdown, the constant intake and build-up of drugs and alcohol in his system contributed to a decline in the quality of his playing and in his band's overall performance.

"Sure, it affected my playing. Of course, my thinking was, Boy, don't that sound good? And there were some great notes that came out, but not necessarily always by my doing. It was kind of like I was getting carried through something. I just wasn't in control; nobody was. We were all exhausted. You could hear it on the tapes of the stuff we had to pull from for the *Live Alive* album. Some of those European gigs were okay; some of them sounded like they were the work of half-dead people."

How, Stevie Ray is asked, was he able to continue as a working artist under such terrible circumstances?

"Part of the deal," he replies, "was that this kind of behavior is so accepted in this industry. It's a classic line: 'Golly, he sure is screwed up, but he sure can play good.' "

Like so many others, Stevie Ray found there were fringe benefits to living the "high" life:

"I found out that if I stayed loaded all the time, my ego got patted on the back and I didn't have to worry about things that I should've been thinking about. It was a lot more comfortable to run from responsibilities. There were a lot of things I was running from and one of them was me. I was a 33-year-old with a six-year-old kid inside of me, scared and wondering where love is."

Charlie Parker, Jimi Hendrix, Jaco Pastorius—all were musical geniuses who drowned their fears and sorrows and anger in drugs and drink. Stevie Ray came perilously close to sharing their terrible fate. "But I didn't have the nuts to do it all the way," he confesses. "And I had a lot of help and support from people, so I was able to see my problem. I came to realize that the alcohol problem, the drug problem and the fear were all symptoms of an underlying problem that's called 'lack of love.' Once you really become an addict or an alcoholic, the drink and drugs just take the place of people you care about and of those people who care about you. You forget how to love—you reject love. You become consumed by fear.

"I was walking around trying to act cool, like I had no fear at all. But I was afraid—afraid that somebody would find out just how scared I was.

"Now I'm finally realizing that fear is the opposite of love."

These days, when Stevie Ray sings "Ain't Gone 'N' Give Up on Love" in concert, the song holds a new, deeper meaning for him. And when he comes to the verse "Love's not gonna give up on me," he's quick to add: "or you!" Having seen the light, he's spreading the message, reaching out to those hordes of guitar freaks and blues lovers who have loyally followed and admired him.

"The music, to me, has become really important. All along, there have been good reasons to play—I like it, a lot of other people like it, it's fun. But beyond that, it can help us out in all kinds of ways. Music really is a way to reach out and hold on to each other in a healthy way. I'm finding that out now. It's helped me to open up more and take a chance on loving people, instead of just isolating and suspecting everybody that I run into."

A smile breaks across his somber face as he adds, "There's just a lot more reason to live now. I can't blame the music for what I got into. I had just kind of misplaced what was really going on with my life. There were a lot of mistakes made and now I can try and learn from those. It took all the crap I went through to come out on this side and now I can try to make amends wherever I can. I've been sober now for 18 months and six days, counting today. I'm discovering that it's really a wonderful world out there; I just have to open my eyes to it."

During his month-long stay in the treatment facility, Stevie Ray was able to slow down, take stock of himself and begin building a new, healthier life. But the battle is far from over, as he explains.

"To show you how crazy this disease of alcoholism is, on the way to the treatment center I borrowed 10 dollars from my mother, telling her I was going to buy some duty-free cigarettes. Instead, I went straight to the bar and spent all the money as quick as I could on double shots of Crown, because I realized that I had never been on a plane sober before. Here I had just come out of the clinic in London, had gotten some information about what was wrong with me, learned all about what the problem was and how to deal with it and still fell right back into that old thinking. I mean, I was on my way to go into a treatment facility, yet my first thought was, Wow, I've never done this straight before. That's the type of thinking that we alcoholics have to defend against for the rest of our lives, though we take it one day at a time. Take care of today—that's the idea."

While in the Marietta treatment facility, Stevie Ray was visited by friends who'd been pulling for him all along. "I had tremendous amounts of support," he sighs. "I still do, from people in the band, the road crew, my mother, my girlfriend, other people who were in the program themselves. A lot of people wrote, called and gave support, because they had gone through things like this. Those people saved my life and now every day that I live, it never fails—somewhere along the line, in the course of a day, I get reminded about those people."

"I had to reach the bottom before I could see clearly."
—STEVIE RAY VAUGHAN

Jackson Browne is one of those people. He first met Stevie Ray in 1982, at the Montreux Festival in Switzerland before the Texas blues man had a record deal. Stevie Ray's blues prowess so impressed Browne that he invited him and his band to use his home studio at no cost. The two remained friendly through the success of *Texas Flood* ('83), *Couldn't Stand the Weather* ('84), *Soul to Soul* ('85) and *Live Alive* ('86). And when Stevie Ray finally crashed, his old pal Jackson was there with a helping hand.

Another visitor to the treatment facility was Eric Clapton, himself no stranger to the evils of self-abuse. Clapton had tried counseling Stevie Ray about his drinking problem years earlier, but as Vaughan recalls, "Back then he could sense that I wasn't ready, so he didn't push it. See, you can try, you can let somebody know what's going on, but if they're not ready, you can't make 'em quit. They're gonna despise you for it and resent the fact that you tried to tell them how to live their life. People in that situation get defensive, they try to act tough and convince themselves, 'Oh, they don't know what they're missing.' And they die inside that way. They really want to say, 'I need help,' but don't know how anymore."

Clapton met Stevie Ray a few years ago, when both were touring Australia. "He was leaving the hotel and I went out to talk to him, hangover and all. He was sober, of course and was really calm the whole while I sat there downing two, three shots of Crown. And he just sort of wisely looked at me and said, 'Well, sometimes you gotta go through that, don'tcha?' If I had been ready to stop then and there, he would've gone on with the next part of it—but he understood that I wasn't. I wouldn't reach that point until I was literally falling off stages, about a couple of years later."

One man who tried to set Stevie Ray straight along the way was blues hero and father-figure Albert King.

"He's someone I've respected all my life, somebody I've looked up to musically and as a person. In fact, there were several times when he said he was like my Daddy. He tried to talk to me on several occasions, but I never listened. Why? Because I was hooked, man. I had to learn for myself. I had to reach the bottom before I could see clearly.

"One time in particular," he says of Albert, "we were doing a show together and he walked in backstage and said, 'We gonna have a heart-to-heart. I been watching you wrestle with that bottle three, four times already. I tell you what, man: I like to drink a little bit when I'm at home. But the gig ain't no time to get high.'

"He was trying to tell me to take care of business, to give myself a break, but I did my usual deal of trying to act like I had it all together, you know? 'Hey, ain't nuthin' wrong, man. I'm leading the life,' and all that bullshit. I was trying not to see it, but I realize now that it's like this: I don't drink or get high because I have all these problems; I have all these problems because I drink and get high. I realize now that nothing's so bad that getting drunk or getting high is gonna make it any better. Period."

He laughs aloud and adds, "Man, sobering up really screws up your drinking. And for that I'm real grateful."

STEVIE RAY, A WHITE PLUME in his black Zorro hat fluttering behind him, plays "Pride and Joy" and does the stroll across the huge stage of Fort Lauderdale's Sunrise Music Theater. It's a little crowd-pleasing trick he may have picked up from fellow-Texan Albert Collins. He beams as he comps on his beat-up old '59 Strat, raking the strings in smooth, circular motions to accentuate the shuffle groove. On the slow blues of "Texas Flood," he digs for roots, dipping deeply into the Albert King bag, just as Jimi Hendrix did on "Red House" and a host of other tunes.

On Howlin' Wolf's "Tell Me," Stevie Ray reaches for some of the raunch of Hubert Sumlin—or Lowell Fulson or Jimmy Rogers. And on "Mary Had a Little Lamb," he pulls out the smooth, fleet-fingered licks that made Buddy Guy a guitar hero. He pays tribute to Freddy King with the classic instrumental "Hideaway," before launching into his own hard-rocking "Scuttle Buttin'," stretching each tune to 10 searing minutes or more.

Stevie Ray is a bit hoarse this night, so he tries to preserve his voice as much as possible. Backstage before the show, he had a certified massage therapist work him over with a little shiatsu on the back of the neck, to loosen up those tight muscles and alleviate strain on the voice box. "I've got an acupuncturist who does wonders for me," he says, "but he's back in New York. He won't travel, so I gotta do what I can on the road."

After a rousing shuffle blues version of the Beatles' "Taxman," Stevie Ray introduces special guest Otis Rush. The Chicago blues man, another boyhood hero of Vaughan's, steps onto the Sunrise stage toting his trusty righty Gibson Stereo 345 (which he flips over and plays lefty, à la Albert King and Jimi Hendrix). The two guitarists have not rehearsed together and Rush barely had time for a sound check. He's playing through a Marshall stack and his semi-hollow Gibson feeds back terribly through the first couple of songs, until the soundmen finally zero in on the proper EQ adjustments.

Stevie and Otis jump into a mid-tempo shuffle. Otis is warming up now and the crowd is clearly warming up to him. By the time he lays into "Stormy Monday," he has this auditorium of young blues fans in the palm of his hand. Many in the crowd have probably never heard of him before, but after a blazing rendition of "Got My Mojo Working," they're well-acquainted with the man. Some will no doubt follow up this first encounter with a trip to the record store and head straight for the blues bins.

And for this, Stevie Ray Vaughan deserves all the credit in the world. He is the premier figure in today's blues world; his drawing power at the box office is even greater than that of B.B. King. But Stevie Ray reveres his blues fathers—B.B., Albert, Freddy and Earl King, Albert Collins, Otis Rush, Buddy Guy, Hubert Sumlin, Jimmy Rogers—the list goes on and on. And, whenever possible, he goes out of his way to repay his debt to them. The wild cheering for Otis Rush at the Sunrise Music Theater reflects—and is the outgrowth of—Stevie Ray's gratitude.

It is boundless. At this year's New Orleans Jazz Heritage Festival, Stevie Ray brought out special guest Albert Collins and the two exchanged licks well into the night. At the Chicago Blues Festival a couple of years back, he mixed it up onstage with the great Buddy Guy. And down around his home stomping grounds, the Austin-Dallas-Fort Worth network, he regularly goes toe-to-toe with the local celebrity six-stringers.

It's all a matter of personal and musical responsibility, says Stevie Ray. "Those guys are the ones who really ought to have the recognition," he maintains. "They're the pioneers and the innovators and they deserve respect for that. All the great records by Albert King and Albert Collins, Otis Rush, B.B. King's *Live at the Regal*—there's millions we could talk about and each one of them is unbelievable in its own right. They're like books, in a sense. You can re-read them and gain a new insight each time. They never sound the same—not to me anyway. There's always something new to learn in each one. So these great blues men, they've all been like my teachers.

"I think I've got something special to say with my music. But I have to keep these things in perspective, because they're gifts. It's all a gift and I have to keep giving it back or it goes away. If I start believing that it's all my doing, it's gonna be my undoing. And I'm committing myself to doing the most I can with the gifts I have, so that they do as many people as much good as possible."

Stevie Ray has stopped running from himself. He's been through some rough times and now he's all the stronger for it—physically, mentally, spiritually and musically. You can hear it in his voice when he sings. You can hear it in his solos. All the crutches have been removed, leaving...the new and improved Stevie Ray Vaughan.

"And now I realize that it's my responsibility to stay sober and to reach out to anybody who's got a problem with it. If I'm in a position to give any kind of help to them and don't, then what have I done? Hell, if it hadn't been for people reaching out to me, I may not have made it."

He pauses, sets his last cup of coffee on the table and points to a small, white lapel-pin bearing the familiar, frizzy-haired visage of Jimi Hendrix.

"You know," he begins urgently, "there's a big lie in this business—that it's okay to go out in flames. But that really doesn't do anybody much good. I may be wrong, but I think Hendrix was trying to come around. I think he had gotten a glimpse of what he needed to change and that he really wanted to change. And I found myself in a similar position."

His voice drops to a solemn whisper as he adds, "Some people can be examples about going ahead and growing. And some people, unfortunately, don't make it there and end up being examples because they had to die. I hit rock-bottom, but thank God my bottom wasn't death."

[6]

"Some of my favorite things to play
started as mistakes."
—*STEVIE RAY VAUGHAN*

STEP BY STEP

A sober SRV discusses his new album, *In Step*.

BY ANDY ALEDORT

THE STEVIE RAY VAUGHAN of this interview, which took place just before the release of *In Step*, was markedly different from the SRV of old. Sobriety had put him more in touch with his innermost feelings, brought him face to face with his greatest fears and weaknesses. Kicking drugs and alcohol had given him the opportunity to have, in his words, a "new life." This was a more serious Stevie Ray, one intent on using the media to transmit the lessons he'd learned to anyone who would listen and, more importantly, those who most needed to.

All the seriousness did not, however, drown out the vibrant enthusiasm that had always been so much a part of his character. Now he greeted people with bear hugs strong enough to crush a Sequoia tree. And when he spoke, he looked right into your eyes. Stevie had become a man determined not to waste any opportunity to communicate.

GUITAR WORLD How long has it been since you recorded the last studio album, *Soul to Soul*?

STEVIE RAY VAUGHAN Four years. We cut *Soul to Soul* in May of '85.

GW Why has it taken four years to record another studio album?

VAUGHAN I guess the world had to turn around a few times, and so did I.

GW How has playing music changed for you since you came out of drug rehabilitation?

VAUGHAN I thought the hardest thing would be, "Oh God, now I'm straight—can I still play?" But that had nothing to do with it. The hardest part is trying to keep things in perspective. I found out that the biggest problem that I had was self-centeredness and ego. That's really what my addiction seems to boil down to. [*chuckles*] To keep that part of myself under control while everybody's telling you how great you are is quite a task.

GW It must be very difficult to see what's really going on without being swayed by what people tell you.

VAUGHAN Yeah. Finding some kind of perspective is the hardest part, because I want to stay alive and I want to stay as healthy as possible, and grow in that way. And while it's getting a lot easier in some ways, every time I think I've learned something, I realize that I've just uncovered a big hole! [*laughs*] A big empty spot, or one that's going, "ARGHHH!"

GW Being a blues musician is about expressing your feelings, and communicating them to the audience. How has the emotional upheaval you've experienced affected you as a musician?

VAUGHAN One thing I've noticed is that songs I used to sing at people, I should have been singing at myself. At least I think that way.

GW Do you hear the words more now?

VAUGHAN Oh God, yeah. Songs mean different things than I used to think they did, too. To put it mildly, a lot of blues tunes have to do with resentments, big time. [*laughs*] Take "Cold Shot." I used to sing that at certain women that I've been involved with over the years. Even though I didn't write it, I had in my head the way I related to it. Since I sobered up, I realized that I left; I was the one who gave the cold shot. And it hurts when you realize that you've hurt somebody, as opposed to, all this time, you've been telling yourself how bad they hurt you. A lot of times, if I stop and look at it, those words could really be telling me that I hurt myself. There are also other songs that are kinder than I thought. They make me feel better than I knew.

> "It hurts when you realize that you've hurt somebody."

GW What are you finding there that makes it feel so good?

VAUGHAN A whole new world. A whole new chance for myself. More so than ever, if I don't play the best that I possibly can and really try to play better than I think I can, then I've wasted it. Because I'm playing on borrowed time. Left to my own devices, I would have killed myself, however slowly or whatever. Now I have a new chance. My best thinking just about killed me, okay? It just so happens that I'm not dead! [*laughs*] Somebody else helped me to stay alive—I just allowed it to happen.

GW How did you manage to capture those feelings on the new record?

VAUGHAN Most of the time, the whole band played together live. It was kind of a difficult record to make. We had fun, but we started and stopped a lot because I was having amp problems.

GW What happened to the amps you used on *Soul to Soul*?

VAUGHAN They weren't holding up. I'd turn 'em on, set them to a real good sound, turn them off to let them cool down, and when it was time to play I'd turn 'em back on and one of them would die. They would either start going, "ACKHHKHK" or "BLLPPPP" or blow up. [*laughs*] I'd hit a couple of notes and it would start making horrible noises. The setup changed from day to day. The amps were dying like flies. This sounds crazy, but I took 32 amps with me. If worse comes to worse, I thought, there'll always be something I can pull out of a road case. I'm glad I took so many amps, because we ended up having only about three or four that worked. In fact, I ended up buying an old '59 Fender Bassman that ended up being my main amp for the whole album. I loved it! It was the one amp that stayed right the whole time. All these new-fangled custom amps I had kept falling apart.

But perhaps the weirdest part of recording this album was that I had to stand in this thing that looked like a square baseball backstop, made out of chicken wire, while I played my parts. There was either a radio station or some kind of microwave stuff that came through the studio—you'd be playing along, and all of a sudden there'd be these weird clicks and buzzes coming out of the amps—but if I stood inside this cage that they made, it wouldn't happen. They caged me! [*laughs*]

GW What other amps did you end up using?

VAUGHAN Usually, I had one Dumble, one Marshall, the Bassman and a Super Reverb. I ran them all at the same time, but they were miked differently and set differently. Sometimes, I ran the effects through them—when I say effects, I'm not talking about space stations, I'm talking about a Fuzz Face, a Tube Screamer or a wah-wah pedal. I also had a Leslie in another room.

GW Stevie Wonder is an example of an artist who has been able to write great music that also carries a message, which is a hard thing to do. I think you've done it very successfully with the songs on this record; the last thing you'd want to do is to sound "preachy."

VAUGHAN No, I really don't want that. It seems real important to me to write about that stuff. I spent so long with this...[*lets out a long, slow exhale*]...image of, "I'm cooler than so-and-so because I get higher than he does." And I really believed it for a long time. But it's just not true.

GW Life doesn't have to be an Iron Man contest.

VAUGHAN No, it doesn't! [*laughs*] And I'd just as soon spend the rest of these years making it clear that it's not true.

GW Was it hard to get these feelings down in a song?

VAUGHAN I went back and forth between feeling really strongly about it and wondering if anybody really wants to hear this shit or not. I knew that I meant it, that I felt good about it sometimes. I was afraid that I'd turn people off. Somewhere along the line that stopped mattering because, with what I was trying to say, if they got turned off, it'd only be for a temporary time. I've been there before, when somebody would try to tell me that I had a problem. I'd go [*in a growl*], "Of course I do! God damn it, don't you think I know that?" I just had to come to grips with it.

GW How did you develop your soloing style?

VAUGHAN It's a real weird mixture. It's kind of everything from my generation to Muddy Waters at the same time. It goes back to my brother Jimmie, when he was bringing home all these different records. Maybe it was because I was a little kid, but it seemed like he brought home The Bluesbreakers with Eric Clapton, Howlin' Wolf, B.B. King, Muddy Waters and the Beatles—all at the same time. It was like, "Here comes Jimmie with the record world!" [*laughs*]

GW The whole history of recorded music was under his arm!

VAUGHAN Yeah! And he knew what he was doing. At the same time, the son of some friends of my parents would come over with his guitar, and he'd show us Jimmy Reed stuff. Here's all this going on, and then somewhere real soon down the line, Jimmie brings home this Jimi Hendrix record, and we both went, "AHHHH! What's this?!"

GW Was it *Are You Experienced*?

VAUGHAN That, and a 45, I think. All at the same time, there were all these different influences. By the time I was 12, Jimmie was gone. Here he was, the hottest guitar player I knew of, and was considered the hottest guitar player in Texas at age 15. I think he started playing when he was 12. [*laughs*]

GW Wasn't he called "Freddie King, Jr." when he was 15?

VAUGHAN Yeah, he was. I mean, what do you do but get excited when all this is going on? If you want to know what made me go crazy with it, it was watching Jimmie. Not trying to out-do him, but, shit, what do you do but pick up the ball and run? It wasn't trying to pass him, and it wasn't trying to keep up with him. It was more like, "Wow! Look what big brother stumbled onto!" A lot of people seem to think that we're trying to beat each other at something, but it's not that at all. I saw him get real exciting—not just excited, but exciting—with something, and that excited me. I didn't know what else to do!

GW What were some of the slow blues you heard that helped you develop your style?

VAUGHAN Albert King records, for one thing. B.B. King's *Live at the Regal*, Albert King's *Born Under a Bad Sign*, it was called first, or *King of the Blues Guitar*. Believe it or not, I remember seeing Albert King on TV, doing "Born Under a Bad Sign," and I was like, "YES!!!"

GW What is it about the blues that makes it so vital and powerful?

VAUGHAN It just sounds more like "the real thing" than anything else. Like I said, it's not [*in a dry, monotone*], "This is cooler than this," or "This has more emotion." When I heard the blues, it killed me, it slayed me! There was just no question. I heard it all these different ways, from the English blues boom to authorized recordings to shitty bootleg stuff of everybody you can dream of. It's funny, because I don't like that there are bootlegs of me out there, but I'm glad I got to hear everyone else's!

GW Have your feelings for the blues changed over the years?

VAUGHAN In recent years, I feel like I've gotten more in touch with it. It's usually when I go and see somebody play who's used to playing clubs, and isn't used to running around in a fancy tour bus and playing arenas.

GW Can you hear that quality in your own playing when you listen back to the tape?

VAUGHAN Sometimes, and it makes me feel good—because I know that I'm still alive.

GW The solo on "Wall of Denial" is one of your best; you don't hold back at all.

VAUGHAN I was jumping up and down! It was real important to us. We had fun on that, man. We had trouble with this and that on the record, but we had fun, too. I learn tricks every once in a while—ways to do things. For that solo I used a Leslie, but it was noisy on the slow speed. So I took a Variac, put it on the slow speed, and then put the

Leslie on the fast speed, making the Leslie go a little faster than slow, without making any clunking noises as it went around.

GW Did you use your Number One guitar for most of *In Step*?

VAUGHAN No, just some of it. I used the white Strat body with a Telecaster neck on some of it. I used the butterscotch one, which is a '61. On "Wall of Denial" I used Number One.

GW That guitar has such a unique sound; it's like a growl.

VAUGHAN I know! But I can't use it all the time because, for some reason, the low E wants to rattle real bad. I had to change the neck; I took the neck off the butterscotch one and put it on Number One. I still have the original neck. For years, Rene [*Martinez, Stevie's guitar tech*] had been taking the frets out, filling the fret slots in, and then putting new frets in. Over time, the slots got too big; it's mainly on the edges. I've been using big frets for so long, it only made it worse.

The original neck has also been broken up by the headstock, which doesn't help. Have you ever seen Jimmie throw his guitar? I learned this trick from him, except his guitar never broke! [*laughs*] I was playing in Lubbock back in '81, and when I threw it, it hit this paneled wall, catching it up by the headstock, snapping the wood. It laid there on the ground, and some of the strings went up, and some of them went down! It was doing all this, "BLUBGBBNGBG!" by itself, and I was standing there, going, "Yeah!" [*laughs*] It happened during "Third Stone from the Sun" and it sounded fine, like it was supposed to be there! But I cried later.

GW I understand that most of the basics for *In Step* were cut live. Is that how the band achieved such great interplay?

VAUGHAN Yeah. We were able to watch each other pretty closely. We were set up so that we could play live: Tommy [*Shannon, bass*] had an iso [*isolation*] booth for his amp, but he was in the same room with

Chris [*Layton, drums*]; Reese [*Wynans, keyboards*] had an iso booth for his Leslie, and I had an iso booth for me and my rig. That way I could get some response out of my rig, but I had a window so I could see in the control room on one side of the room and see Chris on the other side of the room. And we'd watch each other. Also, I had a talkback mic, so I could holler, whistle or, if I could remember the words, sing the vocal part. [*laughs*]

GW Was everyone wearing headphones?

VAUGHAN Yeah. We tried to record without headphones, but the main problem is that I play loud.

GW How loud do you play in the studio as compared to a gig?

VAUGHAN Pretty much the same. In some cases quieter, and in some cases louder. Every room sounds different. I'm trying to learn some things about wood, and the characteristics of the sound. Kiva Studios, where we recorded the album, is a completely wooden room—finished wood—and if I wasn't real careful, I would've ended up having a sound that was too dark. In the studio, my Bassman was set so it sounded so crystalline, so clear and high-endy, but when I got it home, it sounded horrible!

Back to what we were talking about: as a rule, this way seemed to be an easier way to record. For one thing, we all had our own separate mix. We each had a little mixing board right next to us so we could make our own headphone mixes. We were all able to watch each other, and that way we were playing to each other and with each other, cueing off each other, so that it was real spontaneous. At the same time, there was good separation because of the iso booths, and the drums were in the big room to get the big sound. And Tommy was in there, too, feeling it with Chris. It worked out real well.

When we did *Soul to Soul*, we had every amp that I owned at the time hooked up. And they were all in the room with us! We also had a huge P.A. in there—it was some ungodly number of watts—with a 30-inch sub-woofer, which we used for monitors! [*laughs*] For amps, I had two Dumbles, a couple of Marshalls, a bunch of Fenders, and then it trailed off to the side. It was kind of like a galaxy of amps—it spread out like the Milky Way! We just had some foam rubber between my amps and the drums.

GW Did that result in the loss of some realistic separation?

VAUGHAN Yeah, it did. We had to go in and dissect things, and take some of the "bleed" out. There was less "bleed" than we thought there would be, but you can hear some ghost vocals on that record. The isolation we used for *In Step* worked better, and I was still next to my rig, so I could get the response.

GW How long did it take to record *In Step*?

VAUGHAN Fifteen weeks, start to finish. That's not counting the writing of the songs. We had a couple of breaks to do different things.

GW How long did *Soul to Soul* take?

VAUGHAN About three months. That's a realistic amount of time. If we get it done faster, great, but I don't like to lock myself into six weeks, you know? Some people spend a real long time in the studio, but I wouldn't want to get stuck like that. You tend to take the songs apart, put 'em back together, and you end up sterilizing them. I've heard of people slaving together four or five 24-track machines, and you have a zillion tracks going at once. I don't see that as a solution, but I like to leave myself room so that I don't feel too pressured. At the same time I don't want to feel like I don't have to do any work because, given the space, I can be a procrastinator. I like a fixed amount of time, within reason. I like to work at a relaxed pace, but I do like to get back out on the road. We didn't have too much of a chance to get out on the road with the songs on this record, until the end.

GW How many extra tunes were there?

VAUGHAN There were five more that we recorded, with two versions of one of them.

GW Were any of these Hendrix tunes?

VAUGHAN No, not this time. There are several that I'm in love with, like "Stepping Stone" and, of course, "The Wind Cries Mary," "Angel" and "Freedom."

GW Once you get going, it's hard to stop.

VAUGHAN Sure is! [*laughs*] I don't know all of them, though. Some of 'em, I know mostly how it goes, which is okay, because it ends up not being just a copy. There are a lot that we'd like to record, but it was important to us that this record shows where we come from, as much as possible. In fact, I was afraid there wasn't enough blues on it. As it turns out, we actually recorded a few more blues tunes that didn't make the record. We recorded "Boot Hill" [*released posthumously on* The Sky Is Crying], and I play slide on the whole thing. It's a Sly Williams song.

I used my Charlie Christian guitar for that, and it sounded horrible—the right kind of horrible. [*laughs*] It was real fat. It sounded like it's supposed to. But, once again, we keep trying to do it in a key that's too high for me to sing. And I should know by now, because we've recorded that song for every record except *Texas Flood*. And we did it too high again! The track does sound real good, though. We'll do it again, in a lower key next time. I've got my Charlie Christian with me on the road now, tuned down to C♯ or C, I forget which one.

GW Is that the key you can sing it in?

VAUGHAN Yeah.

GW "Crossfire" reminds me of some of the Albert King stuff that was recorded at Stax.

VAUGHAN Yeah. The first time I heard that song, it reminded me of Junior Walker a whole lot. I thought it was a neat song, but it was arranged in a slightly different way, and I was uncomfortable playing it. I didn't know what to play! And it was hard to admit that I didn't know what to play. I just said, "This is weird!" [*laughs*]

GW It was the song's fault.

VAUGHAN Yeah. "This song's weird, man!" But then I came to grips with it. I had to let the band carry the riff, and it has taken me a while to learn to let the band carry what they're going to carry anyway, you know? I don't have to be all over everything to make it work.

But there are songs that never get finished. I think of them as babies that never grow up. It's funny, because I went through a grieving process when we were done tracking. I felt bad for the songs that were never completely recorded, so I just sat in my room and played them by myself. I played my babies that never grew up.

GW Did you record anything on the National steel guitar that you're holding in the cover photo?

VAUGHAN Not this time, but I had planned on it. I did record one song, "Life By the Drop," by myself with the 12-string acoustic. I recorded it that way because it sounded more personal. However, the more we worked on it—I did several takes—the more the producer and myself

"I felt bad for the songs that were never completely recorded, so **I just sat in my room and played them by myself.**"

heard it as a band song. I may go in and record it with the guy who wrote it, Doyle Bramhall—the father, not the son.

GW In "Tightrope," there is the lyric, "There was love all around me, but I was looking for revenge. Thank God it never found me, would have been the end." What's that about?

VAUGHAN A lot of times, our fears keep us from seeing what's really there. I realized the other day when I got a glimpse of what life would be like without my fears, without my guilt and my shame—without that club to beat myself over the head with. It was just for a couple of minutes, and I realized that without that stuff...I never realized how much those feelings and those emotions permeate everything. I got a glimpse of how I felt without all of that, and I felt a lot better about everything and everybody. It was a real neat deal. I was just talking to somebody, and they said something that sparked it. It was like being in a completely smoke-filled room—like a cloud—and then somebody turned on a vent and all the smoke was gone for a minute.

I learned all that stuff—the guilt and the shame—when I was a little kid; I learned how to be afraid all the time because it wasn't very "constant" at home. I don't know if everybody else in the family perceived it the same way; probably not. But I learned real quickly not to know what to expect, so therefore I'd just stay out of the way, keep my feelings out of the way. If I did have feelings, it must have been my fault, because that's what I heard when the fights were going on. I didn't realize how deeply that was embedded in me. Without someone else doing it, I do it to myself, because I'm familiar with that, you know? It's a shame.

GW For whatever the reason, that stuff is self-sustaining.

VAUGHAN Uh-huh. I'm just now learning how to let go of some of that, and I can't always do it. Sometimes, I can put the club down. And other times, I pick it right back up and go to flogging myself! [*laughs*] It's an old pattern that I have to learn how to not do.

GW Do those feelings ever come out while you're playing?

VAUGHAN Sometimes they crawl all over me. It happened the other night: We were playing along, and all of a sudden I start feeling all of this self-conscious crap crawling all over me. You just want to tear your skin off and run!

GW It's like a vine crawling up your leg.

VAUGHAN Yeah, except, believe me, it's already all over my head! [*laughs*] And then I opened my eyes and saw all these people watching us, really having a blast, and I thought, What am I doing to myself? These people accept us. I'm the only one who's not accepting myself right now. There's something to always wanting to be better; it gives us a reason to try to grow. But it's not all right to allow myself to be unaccepting of everything. The audience was honestly enjoying what we were doing, and I was sabotaging it! It's an easy thing to do, sometimes. But, in reality, all I have to do is stop and look where I've come from. That has to do with how my life is changing for the better. If I stop and look at where I found myself before I got clean... Where I'm at now is a little better than when I was puking up blood and bile in the middle of the street, and then getting up and going, "Hey man, I think I need a drink."

GW When I saw you at the Pier in New York last summer, there was this relentless intensity to your guitar playing that was just incredible. I had wondered how your problems with drug addiction would affect your playing. What I heard was a tremendous outpouring of good feelings.

VAUGHAN Well, I have to keep trying. And I do. I know that everything is better now, and I do mean everything. My whole life is better. It's hard for me to see that when everything is better, that includes the music, too. There's no reason why it shouldn't. I'm not saying that it's an automatic deal—I have to work at these things harder than ever. And that's fine with me. I'm glad I do. It has to do with progression, and there's healthy and unhealthy sides to it. The balance is the thing to try to find.

GW Do the slide-ups at the beginning of your version of "Love Me Darlin' " come from Hubert Sumlin's playing on the original?

VAUGHAN Yeah. It's just more evident because I've got my Fuzz Face on, and I get more of a ripping sound. Hubert had a real crystal-clear sound, almost too crystal-clear to be true. I've always tried to figure out how in the hell he got that sound. I still haven't gotten it! I've gotten close, but he gets this natural sound.

GW How did the song "Travis Walk" come about?

VAUGHAN We were in a rehearsal hall, working on "Scratch 'N' Sniff," and we couldn't decide what we wanted to do. We stopped for a minute; everybody was real frustrated. I walked over to the corner, looked at this picture of my brother, and jumped into playing the tune! [*laughs*] He just looked so cool in the picture.

GW When you write, do you think at all about the style the tunes are in, or where they're coming from?

VAUGHAN It's just a sound I hear in my head, and a feeling I have. I don't know how to decipher between my thoughts and my feelings and, in a way, that's real good. It's confusing sometimes, when you're trying to weed through 'em, but when I hear something, it makes me feel a certain way. And when I feel something, often I'll hear certain things. Then, I try to act on it in a constructive way, which is to play.

GW On this record, you've brought in some different grooves and different feelings that you haven't in the past, on such songs as "Tightrope," "Crossfire" and "Wall of Denial."

VAUGHAN I keep trying to make it all come out. I can't read or write music, so sometimes, in trying to find things, I just stick my hand on the neck. Sometimes it's a surprise and sometimes it becomes what I wanted to hear. I visualize things—sometimes I visualize correctly, sometimes I don't. As a result, some of my favorite things to play started as mistakes!

GW Speaking of mistakes: I've heard that the live album [*Live Alive*] is something that you're not very happy with.

VAUGHAN Well, God, I wasn't in very good shape. I didn't realize how bad a shape I was in at the time. There were more fix-it jobs done on the album than I would have liked.

GW I think "Texas Flood" is a shining moment on that album.

VAUGHAN That was from the Montreux Jazz Festival, and we felt good about what we were doing. Overall, there were some good nights and some good gigs, but it was more haphazard than we would have liked.

GW What would you put on your "essential listening" list?

VAUGHAN Buddy Guy's *A Man and the Blues* even though he himself doesn't like the record. [*laughs*] B.B. King's *Live at the Regal*, Grant Green's *Live at the Lighthouse*—it's not blues, but it's wonderful—anything by Donny Hathaway, especially the *Donny Hathaway: Live* album; it kills me. There's a lot of gospel stuff that I love, but not necessarily up-to-date stuff. People sometimes turn me on to things that aren't new at all.

Of course, I love a lot of Albert King, but I don't know what my favorite would be. There's all kinds of stuff! Hendrix kind of goes without saying. I like just about everything by him. Keep in mind that I go through phases with all of these people, and phases with what I listen to. It's not that I think one is more important than the other; it has to do with what I can take in. I can't take it all in at once. I haven't been home for a while, and I need to dig back into my records.

REPRINTED FROM *GUITAR WORLD*, AUGUST 2000

[7]

"I looked into Stevie's eyes,
and it was like looking into
the eyes of a dead deer."
—*CHRIS LAYTON*

PRIDE AND JOY

In an interview of unprecedented depth, Double Trouble painstakingly details the euphoric highs and devastating lows of recording and performing with blues guitar genius Stevie Ray Vaughan.

BY ANDY ALEDORT

STEVIE HAD A WAY OF PLAYING that sounded totally different from every other player, because of the spirit he poured into it. The inner dynamic of whatever he was—that *spark*—always shone right through."

These words, spoken by Tommy Shannon, Double Trouble bassist and longtime musical compatriot of Stevie Ray Vaughan, express a point of view shared the world over by blues lovers and guitar players. Stevie Ray possessed a stockpile of ammunition: a searing guitar sound, mercurial technique, gut-wrenching vocals and, most importantly, a fiery intensity and burning musical passion that was simply relentless. No less a musical authority than John Hammond, Sr.—the man who discovered Bessie Smith, Charlie

Christian, Bob Dylan and Bruce Springsteen—described Vaughan in this way: "I haven't heard a musician as imbued with the blues spirit as Stevie since Robert Johnson."

Born October 3, 1954, in Oak Cliff, a Dallas suburb, Vaughan grew up in a household filled with music. His parents had many musician friends, such as members of Bob Wills and the Texas Playboys. And then there was Vaughan's guitar-playing brother, Jimmie, who would in later years earn fame for his brilliant work with the Fabulous Thunderbirds, and would record one album with Stevie, *Family Style*.

Stevie Ray Vaughan began playing guitar at age seven, and gained a vast musical education via his brother's expansive record collection, as well as his brother's daily devotion to mastering the art of blues guitar. The sounds of Jimmy Reed, B.B. King, Chuck Berry, T-Bone Walker, Lightnin' Hopkins, Albert King and Freddie King were diligently consumed. While Jimmie was out, "Little Stevie" would sneak into his brother's room and try to pick up where big brother had left off.

Jimmie also supplied Stevie with lifelong inspiration when he arrived home with a certain piece of vinyl under his arm. "Somewhere down the line," Stevie recalled, "here comes Jimmie with this Jimi Hendrix record—*Are You Experienced?*—and we both went, 'Ahh! What's *this*?!' " Hendrix inspired Stevie more than any other musician; for many years, Stevie proudly carried Jimi's autograph with him wherever he went.

By the age of 12, Stevie was playing in bands like the Epileptic Marshmallow, Liberation and Storm, alongside Jimmie. By 1970, he had proven himself worthy to play with some of Dallas' best musicians. While Stevie was jamming at a local club, Tommy Shannon happened upon the nascent guitar hero: "I had just come off the road with Johnny Winter, and as I was walking up to the club—which is, coincidentally, where I first met Johnny—I could hear the guitar, and it sounded really special to me. I knew, even from those first few notes, that I was hearing something *great*. I expected to see an older guy up there, but there was this scrawny, awkward 15-year-old kid." Tommy and Stevie forged a friendship that night; it wouldn't be long before their paths crossed again.

Stevie dropped out of high school in 1972, moved to Austin, Texas, in pursuit of blues guitar heaven, and never looked back. Soon after, he joined Blackbird. "Blackbird were great, and drew real big crowds," says Shannon. "In the two years that had passed, Stevie's playing had evolved; he was incredible! All of the musicians were saying, 'Man—listen to that guy!' Stevie had so much admiration for the older musicians, but he honestly didn't realize he was already better than most of them."

At the time, Tommy was playing in Krackerjack, one of Austin's hottest bands. When they broke up, Tommy joined Vaughan in Blackbird, followed by the formation of Krackerjack II. When that band broke up, Tommy says, "We went our separate ways, and I began my descent into a drug-filled hell." It wasn't until six years later that Tommy would find his way back into music.

Stevie's next band was the Nightcrawlers and, following a gig in 1973, Vaughan found what would become his most-prized possession: the 1959 Strat he dubbed Number One.

"Stevie walked into Ray Hennig's Heart of Texas Music with this black Strat he'd been playing," says Double Trouble drummer Chris Layton, "and stood looking at the row of guitars on the wall. He said, 'Will you trade me this guitar for...[*slowly moves his finger through the air in a straight line, and then stops, transfixed, like a divining rod*]...that guitar right there!' [*laughs*] He picked up a vibe from that guitar, from all the way across the room!"

Vaughan's next move was monumental, joining the best blues/R&B/soul band in Austin: Paul Ray and the Cobras. It was in this band that Layton first saw Stevie. "In late 1976 or early 1977, I saw Stevie play with Paul Ray and the Cobras out at the original Soap Creek Saloon, in Westlake," he recalls. "A sax player I knew from Corpus Christi, Joe Sublett, had joined the band, and suggested I come and check them out.

"The Cobras played every Tuesday night, and they literally packed the place; you couldn't get in! I could hear the music as I walked up to the club. The rest of the band sounded muffled, but the guitar sounded like the guy was playing outside of the building! It wasn't that it was louder than the rest of the band; Stevie's tone, his groove and his energy was so *right on* that it sounded like he was 'beyond' the band. It stopped me in my tracks; it was that striking. I walked in the door and immediately saw Stevie. He amazed me. No one had ever struck me the way he did." Chris sat in with the Cobras shortly thereafter, and he and Stevie felt an immediate musical affinity.

Though Vaughan didn't read music, both Layton and Shannon describe Stevie as someone blessed with an ear. "Oh, he had a great ear," says Layton. "He wasn't into out-and-out copying things, though. He was interested in capturing the spirit of a song."

It was Vaughan's ability to tap into that spirit and communicate it to the audience that struck Shannon the most. "For Stevie, playing music was a transmission of something deep inside himself. He reached as far down into his heart, his soul and his life as he could reach. If he was in pain, he'd *play* that pain; if he was happy, he'd *play* that happiness. He took that for granted, but it's not a common thing at all."

Chris concurs, adding that Vaughan's playing revealed his true personality. "Stevie *was* that thing that people identify with, that thing they can hear in his music. People say they feel they knew him just from listening to his music. And, in a way, they really did."

In 1977, Vaughan left the Cobras to form Triple Threat Revue, a group that also featured singer Lou Ann Barton, bassist WC Clark, drummer Freddy Pharoah and keyboardist Mike Kindred. By 1978, Kindred and Clark had split, replaced by Johnny Reno on sax and Jack Newhouse on bass. The new band, Double Trouble, had a revolving drum stool soon occupied by Chris Layton. "Stevie came over to our upstairs garage apartment one day while I was playing along with 'What's Going On?' from *Donny Hathaway Live*. I looked down on the floor and I saw feet tapping, and there was Stevie. They needed a drummer, and Stevie said, 'You want to play with me?' and I said, 'Fuck, yeah!' He said, 'C'mon, let's go!' And that was that."

The band, however, was in disarray. Following an infamous row between Vaughan and Lou Ann at New York's Lone Star Cafe, the band dwindled down to a trio of Stevie, Jack and Chris. This is where Tommy Shannon reenters the picture.

"Late in 1980, I went to see them at a place called Rockafeller's, and I had a revelation: I thought, That's where I belong. It was a real powerful feeling, like I'd suddenly woken up. They took a break, and I went up to Stevie and said, 'I belong in this band!' We jammed that night, and it sounded so good. A little while later, I went to see them at Fitzgerald's. I accidentally dropped a piece of broccoli with dip on it in Stevie's lap, and I thought, Well, I blew it! But he called me the next day, and I quit the band I was in on the spot."

The new lineup of Vaughan, Shannon and Layton took on an entirely new musical personality. "When Tommy replaced Jack," says Layton, "there wasn't anyone left to tug at Stevie and say, 'Hey, remember, this is supposed to be the *blues*.' Tommy and I were enthusiastic about lots of other things, and that's when the whole thing really started changing."

With Layton and Shannon, Vaughan had found musicians willing to go wherever he would lead them. "The music was our guide," Shannon likes to say. But breaking away from the pure blues mold—and the deeply instilled influence of brother Jimmie—was not easy for Stevie.

"For a long time, he was afraid of doing Hendrix songs because it would be perceived by the blues purists as 'crossing the boundaries,' " Shannon reveals. "It was something he struggled with." Layton concurs, "There were a bunch of people in Austin very much into the 'blues purist' thing—that's what you were supposed to *strive* to become. Stevie actually ended up as one of the prominent leaders in that scene. To work out of it took a lot of encouragement from us, which we gave him because it was obvious that he liked music that did not only pertain to the blues purist school of thought."

Shannon adds, "The coolest thing was watching that transformation happen, when he finally stepped over that line and became comfortable in that role. That's when he really took off. And it wasn't just about playing Hendrix stuff, because it translated to the way we played blues and everything else. That's when he became the Stevie that everybody knows. He never abandoned the traditional blues, whatsoever; it was in everything we played, but in a new way. He saw that as a whole new sound. That's when he crossed that line and began to really trust his own instincts."

GUITAR WORLD The turning point in the story of Stevie Ray Vaughan and Double Trouble is the band's legendary appearance at the Montreux Jazz Festival in 1982. What events led to that performance?

CHRIS LAYTON Jerry Wexler [*Atlantic Records executive*] made that happen. Lou Ann Barton had a record deal with Elektra/Asylum [Old Enough, *co-produced by Wexler*], and we played at her record release party at the Continental Club in Austin. Wexler saw us play, and loved it. He called Claude Nobs, who ran the Montreux Jazz Festival, and told him that we'd be sensational. So, we were on our way.

GW That show is immortal for a few reasons: one is that you were booed; another is that you ended up winning your first Grammy for "Texas Flood" [*included on the compilation* Atlantic Blues: Guitar, *under the title "Flood Down in Texas"*]; and, most importantly, it's where you hooked up with Jackson Browne and David Bowie.

TOMMY SHANNON It turned out to be the most important gig we ever played. Because of the booing, though, Stevie was brokenhearted.

LAYTON I was bummed, too. It was like, God, we came all the way over here to get booed off the stage?

SHANNON Stevie was so hurt. He said, "I didn't think we sounded *that* bad, did you? We didn't deserve that!" We were all crushed.

The next night, we played downstairs in the musician's bar, all night, until the sun came up. Jackson Browne and his band came down, and they jammed with us. David Bowie was hanging out. It was so much fun—there were no breaks.

LAYTON It lasted all night. We were snortin' and jammin' and havin' a great time. We finally walked out of there at about seven in the morning. The whole two-day experience was a wild circumstance, really.

SHANNON [*To Layton*] How did we get that downstairs gig, anyway?

LAYTON Chesley [*Millikin, the band's manager and president of Classic Management*] set it up. No one was scheduled to play down there, but it was where all of the players hung out before and after they played.

Chesley said, "Let's book ourselves in the musician's bar. There's no telling who'll be there." We thought, Well, fuck, we flew all the way over here—we might as well play. Jackson Browne came in and said, "Hey, who are you guys?" We talked, and we just started jamming. It was really *that* gig that led to everything that followed.

GW Is that where Bowie saw you?

LAYTON I had met him the night before, following our performance on the main stage. I sat and talked with him for about 45 minutes, down in that same bar.

GW Was it at that jam that Jackson invited you to record at his studio, which resulted in the recording of *Texas Flood*?

LAYTON Yes. He had a studio in Los Angeles called Down Town Studios. If he saw a band he liked, he would help them. He mostly did eclectic things—he had just recorded this Native American Indian thing—so it wasn't like he was looking for rock bands. He made the offer to us, saying that if we were ever in Los Angeles and wanted to record in his studio, just let him know and he'd arrange it. We took him up on the offer.

GW Following Montreux, but before you went to Jackson's studio, Chesley had passed a live video of the band's Tornado Jam performance to the Stones, which generated their interest.

SHANNON The Stones had their own record label [*Rolling Stones Records*], and they were considering signing us.

LAYTON Chesley knew Mick [*Jagger*], and Mick had seen the tape. Chesley said, "You've really got to see these guys live." Mick was into it, and he told Chesley when he'd be in New York. We did all of the work to set up that gig at Danceteria, and it was all at our own expense. That was a really bizarre gig.

Danceteria had different things happening all night, with different bands and constant turnover. For one of those segments, we closed the club off and showcased for the Stones. There were only a few people there—Mick Jagger, Ron Wood and whoever else made their way in. We only played a few songs, met them, the photographers took some shots, and then everyone was gone.

GW It sounds like a drive-by.

LAYTON It was a drive-by showcase for Mick Jagger. Supposedly, Mick's comment to the guy running their label was, "I like them, but everybody knows that blues doesn't sell." So they passed.

GW Didn't a photo of Stevie and Mick from that night get published in *Rolling Stone*, which earned the band much-needed publicity?

LAYTON Oh yeah, that's true. [*Legendary publicist*] Charles Comer made that happen. After we played, we went backstage, and here comes Jagger and Ron Wood. As soon as we were all together, 20 photographers jumped into the room and began shooting. Then, just like that, it was over. Chesley got the shot published in *Rolling Stone*, which ended up getting us a lot of attention.

SHANNON The coolest thing was that we were starting to get the attention of people like David Bowie, Jackson Brown, Jerry Wexler and the Rolling Stones. We couldn't help but feel that something good was about to happen.

LAYTON It seemed undeniable at that point. I mean, coming from playing at places like Skipwilly's in San Antonio for four drunks, and all of a sudden, "Oh, we're going to Montreux?" "David Bowie wants Stevie to play on his record, and he wants Double Trouble to open the shows?" Then, Jackson Browne wanted to loan us his studio, and Mick Jagger wanted us to fly to New York to play for him. All these things were happening one after the other. It seemed like there were too many heavy things going on for it to all mean absolutely nothing. All of a sudden, this huge momentum was beginning to build.

TEXAS FLOOD (1983)

GW On the Thanksgiving weekend of 1982, you went to Jackson Browne's studio to record *Texas Flood*.

SHANNON We did the whole record in just three days: we didn't get anything the first day, got two songs the second day and eight songs the third. We set up the same way as we did live: Stevie was on one side with his amps, I was on the other side with mine, and the drums were in the middle.

GW Was *Texas Flood* the first time Stevie used a Dumble amp, which became a major ingredient in his signature sound?

LAYTON It was. The Dumble was Jackson's amp—it was called Mother Dumble. Stevie loved it, and said, "I've got to get one of these!"

GW Were you guys excited about the recording?

LAYTON Not really. It was like playing a gig in a warehouse with no one there. It wasn't really like working on a record, because it was so "live."

SHANNON Stevie was very proud of it, though, because he liked the sound we got. In the middle of the song "Testify," we "punched in" the entire band! [*"Punch in" is a term for when a recording engineer sets a tape machine into "record" mode while the tape is running—Ed.*] Stevie had broken a string, and it was such a good take up to that point, he wanted to keep it. We rolled up to that point, and then we continued from there, punching in the entire band. And it worked.

GW Many SRV fans cite *Texas Flood* as their favorite record, because of the immediacy and freshness in the sound.

SHANNON Stevie said that we had waited all of our lives to make that first record. After that, making records was work.

GW Can you detail the origin of the tunes on *Texas Flood*?

LAYTON "Pride and Joy" and "I'm Crying" are basically the same song but with different lyrics; "Pride and Joy" went back to the mid-Seventies when he was living with his girlfriend, Lindi Bethel. "Love Struck Baby" was a song that he'd written for his wife, Lenny, as well as the song "Lenny." Each girl had two songs, so he was keeping it even!

"Dirty Pool" is a song that went all the way back to the Nightcrawlers. We recorded it with a guy named Joe Gracey in an early incarnation of Double Trouble. Same with "Rude Mood." "Texas Flood" and "Tell Me" were songs we'd been doing in clubs. "Testify" is an old Isley Brothers song that we started to do when Tommy got in the band.

We didn't know we were making a record, so we basically played all the songs we had been playing at the gigs. We'd record something, listen to it, and if it sounded good, we'd go on to the next song.

GW Did David Bowie call Stevie while you were recording the album?

LAYTON He called our apartment at 3:30 in the morning. I answered the phone, and this quiet English voice said, "Is Stevie Vaughan there?" I said, "Damn, who is this?" "This is David Bowie." I'm thinking, You mean, the Thin White Duke? Ziggy Stardust? [*laughs*]

GW What was Stevie's reaction to receiving this call?

SHANNON He was really excited about being asked to play on Bowie's record. At that point, he thought we were going to open the shows, because that's what Bowie told him.

LAYTON That was part of the original pitch. It was presented as, "Stevie should come and play on my record, and I'm planning a world tour. It would be great if Double Trouble opened the shows." But it was really an insinuation as opposed to a real invitation. Obviously, it didn't happen.

GW The point was, you can come tour with me and you won't have to leave your band on the sidelines for a year.

LAYTON David's a pretty smart guy. It was a way to get Stevie interested in the whole thing.

SHANNON Stevie was pissed off when he found out that they didn't really want us to open the shows. That came to light fairly late in the game, after he'd done the recording for *Let's Dance* and begun rehearsing for the tour. Meanwhile, Chesley was pressuring Stevie tremendously: "Stevie, you've got to do this tour with Bowie!"

GW March 1983 was when the rehearsals took place for the tour. Something happened that caused Bowie to insist that Chesley relinquish his managerial control over Stevie until the tour was over.

LAYTON The *Dallas Morning News* had run this big cover story on Stevie called "Dallas' Favorite Son." There was a picture of Stevie on the front of the entertainment section that was huge, with a little tiny picture of Bowie. Lenny felt that Stevie wasn't getting his due for the tour, and she went to the rehearsal with the paper. Right in the middle of the rehearsal, at the end of a song, she walked up to Bowie and threw the paper down at his feet. She said, "Look at that!"

> "Stevie hated it when someone tried to control him."
> —*CHRIS LAYTON*

Right after that happened, Bowie insisted that he orchestrate all and any press that had to do with Stevie Ray Vaughan's career inside Bowie's organization and outside of it, too. He was turning the screw a little tighter. But Stevie hated it when someone tried to control him. That made him want to break out of jail that much more, so to speak.

SHANNON We didn't have shit going for us as a band at that time. We had *Texas Flood* in the can, but no deals were in sight. After bailing out of the Bowie tour, Stevie had nothing to return to other than driving around in the band van, which was a milk truck.

LAYTON Right around that time, John Hammond, Sr. put the wheels in motion to get us a deal. He went to CBS, and Epic decided to sign us. In actuality, by the time Stevie bailed on the Bowie tour, we were close to signing with Epic.

GW How close to the beginning of the tour did Stevie bail out?

LAYTON The day before they we supposed to leave for Brussels. Funny as it may sound, we weren't really that surprised. Knowing Stevie, and from all of the talks we had had, it was clear that, all of his life, all he wanted to have was his own band and play his own music. He felt confident that he was finally going to be able to do the things he'd been waiting his whole life to do.

GW What was the management's reaction to his decision?

SHANNON They thought he was out of his fucking mind. There weren't many people telling him that he'd made the right decision! [*laughs*] Except us! The fact that he bailed out when he did was a scandalous thing, for a time. What it came down to was that Stevie couldn't do what he couldn't put his heart into. Most guitarists, no matter who they were, would have gone and played the game and worked for their career. Stevie always came in the back door, never the front. That was his approach to life.

GW By the time *Let's Dance* came out, the Epic deal was in place, correct?

LAYTON Yeah. These events followed each other fairly quickly.

SHANNON The three of us were playing this club, and the "Let's Dance" video came on the TV. Davie Bowie was pretending to play all of Stevie's guitar parts, and Stevie got so pissed off! He was furious.

LAYTON Stevie said, "That motherfucker shouldn't be pretending to be playing shit he wasn't playing!"

SHANNON Stevie had passed up the chance to get in limos everyday, and fly all over the world. Instead, he chose the milk truck.

GW He must have believed very strongly in what he had at home.

SHANNON Exactly. And it was meant to be, because everything started to happen right after that. The coolest thing is what happened when *Texas Flood* came out. Epic hadn't done any huge promotion at all, but people were buying our record in droves through word of mouth.

I knew something was happening when we drove all the way to California for a gig at the Palace in Hollywood. As we were pulling up to the club, there was a line all the way around the block.

LAYTON That fucker was sold out! And the record had only been out for a few weeks! It was like that everywhere we went after that. The 400-seaters were sold out, but the Palace held 2,000 people, and it was sold out too.

SHANNON That was the first big indication that something was happening, right there, that night. It was a hallmark in the momentum of our career. After that, we switched booking agents, from Joe Priesnitz to Alex Hodges, and he put us on tour with the Moody Blues.

The first gig was at the Meadowlands in New Jersey—21,000 people! The best word I can think of to describe that tour is "glorious." Our record hadn't become that successful yet, but we were playing in front of coliseums full of people. We just went out and played, and it fit like a glove. The sound rang through those big coliseums like a monster. People were going crazy, and they had no idea who we were.

GW How did this newfound success affect Stevie?

SHANNON He was very excited and happy. It was an affirmation, not only for Stevie but for all of us. We found out that what we loved—what we had put our life and soul into—other people loved, too. We started getting calls: "The record's taking off! It's doing great!" All of these great offers were coming in, and all these different people were coming out to see us. At our own shows, we started drawing bigger and bigger crowds and playing bigger and bigger places. That validation by so many people gave us more strength to really take off.

GW Did that excitement get translated into the music?

SHANNON The validation by so many people brought us to a higher level—things were happening, and that much more started coming out of us, in terms of our musical energy. We started growing. We got used to the big stages, and how to handle it. It felt so right, like we knew that we belonged up there.

The unspoken rule in the band was that, when we got onstage, everyone was expected to put every ounce of life into what we were doing; nothing less was acceptable. If anyone slacked for a split second, the other guys would pick up on it. To slack off at that point, after all that we had been through, would have been like spitting on God.

GW Reese, do you remember the first time you heard Stevie play live?

REESE WYNANS I sure do. It was at the Continental Club, shortly after *Texas Flood* came out, in 1983. I had been wanting to hear him for a long time. The place was so crowded, you couldn't even get in the door! They had speakers set up outside, and a closed-circuit TV so everyone outside could hear the music and see the band.

SHANNON We were so loud, big chunks of the ceiling were falling down!

WYNANS It was loud as hell. I thought, These guys are fantastic! You could go inside and see nothing, or you could go outside and watch the band on the TV, and hear them out of these big speakers. It was a more reasonable volume outside, anyway. [*laughs*]

I also saw you guys at the Steamboat at least once. Back then, everyone talked about, "What do they play better, the blues or the Hendrix stuff?" "I think they should just play the blues." "No, I think they should do the rock stuff!" I thought, Stick with what you're doing, because it's pretty good!

COULDN'T STAND THE WEATHER (1984)

[*Hanging out at Flipnotics, a laid-back, indoor/outdoor club in South Austin*]

GW By the end of 1983, *Texas Flood* was certified Gold. In January of 1984, you went to the Power Station in New York to record *Couldn't Stand the Weather*.

LAYTON That was like, "party down, man!" Big record budget, living at the Mayflower Hotel in New York City, drinking, snortin' cocaine. John Hammond was sitting in on the sessions. He'd come in his tweed coat, bowtie, sack lunch and *New York Times*. He'd sit down, read the paper and make a comment here and there about the groove or whatever.

We were doing a lot of drugs then. We thought, We can't do drugs in front of John Hammond! So, we'd go sneak off behind the Steinway piano. One time, we came back into the control room after sneaking off, and John is sitting there with the paper. He closes it and sets it in his lap, and then looks off, like he's going to be real reflective.

He says, "Years ago, I worked with Gene Krupa. Fabulous drummer—incredible musician! One of the greatest. He had this thing, though, that he liked to do from time to time. He loved to smoke pot. And when he did, his timing went all to shit. He became something unlike what he really was when he smoked that marijuana. Even since then, I just don't like drugs in my sessions." And he picked up his paper and started reading again! We were all speechless.

GW What are the origins of the tunes on *Couldn't Stand the Weather*?

SHANNON The title tune took a while to come together. One day, I was playing a bass lick similar to the funky R&B line at the beginning of the song, and Stevie dug it and changed it around a bit. The rest of the song grew from there, but it took quite a while to take shape. Stevie spent a long time on the lyrics, too.

LAYTON "Cold Shot" was a tune that Mike Kendrid of Triple Threat had written. When we cut the tune, I had been sleeping on the couch— I was out cold. Stevie ran in and woke me up, saying, "C'mon, man, we gotta play!" The fact that I was so sleepy had a major effect on the slow, loping groove of that song.

"Tin Pan Alley" was another one that Stevie loved and we had been doing for quite a while. That was actually the first tune we cut for the record. We were in the studio getting sounds, and Stevie said, "Why don't we just go ahead and play something?" So we played "Tin Pan Alley," sort of as a warm-up. When we were done, John Hammond said, "You'll never get it better than that." And he was right.

GW Stevie had said that "Scuttle Buttin' " was based on the Lonnie Mack tune "Chicken Feed."

LAYTON It was really based on Lonnie Mack's style. "The Things (That) I Used to Do" was cool because Jimmie [*Vaughan*] came in to play on it. He played some amazing rhythm guitar on that song, more like a keyboard player than a guitar player. "Honey Bee" is a song Stevie wrote for the record. "Stang's Swang" was cut with the Fabulous Thunderbirds drummer, Fran Christina. I think I was out somewhere, or unconscious!

GW Did Stevie have any reservations about putting "Voodoo Child (Slight Return)" on the record?

LAYTON No. We were feeling pretty damn good by that point. *Texas Flood* had done great, and we had this big budget and were camped out in New York City. We felt like we could do whatever we wanted.

GW When *Couldn't Stand the Weather* was released, it sold 250,000 copies in 21 days. That's more than 10,000 records a day.

LAYTON A lot of that was in Texas and in the southwest—Arizona, Oklahoma and New Mexico.

GW All through 1983, you went back and forth between appearing as a headliner for a major act and headlining yourself. Any particular recollections of that tour?

LAYTON At that time, every night was an event. We were flipping out about all of it. Besides the shows, we were doing press and radio interviews every day. It was a whirlwind.

GW On October 3, 1984, Stevie celebrated his 30th birthday. The next day, the band played a historic concert at Carnegie Hall, released as *Live at Carnegie Hall.*

SHANNON It was a dream for him to play Carnegie Hall, and he went to all lengths to make that show happen. We had these special clothes made just for the gig, the mariachi suits.

LAYTON We went to Nella's tailors up on Airport Boulevard, and they had all kinds of cool silver buttons and buckles. We said, "We want these on our pants, and these for the buttons on the jackets." They showed us all of this material, and Stevie had two suits—a blue and a red—and we were in blue.

An elaborate stage set was built out of plywood and 2x4s and painted lapis blue enamel with gold lamé striping on it. They shipped it to New York, set it up in a warehouse, and we did one dress rehearsal.

The next day, it was broken down and brought over to Carnegie Hall and reconstructed.

SHANNON We got all of the special guests, like Dr. John, Jimmie Vaughan, Angela Strehli, the Roomful of Blues horns and George Rains, and brought them to a soundstage in Austin called Third Coast. We rehearsed for three days and had everyone fitted for their clothes.

SHANNON We played two "warm-up" shows in Forth Worth at the Caravan of Dreams, which was a beautiful, brand-new facility then. The crowds were great, the shows were great.

LAYTON Then we were off to New York, the dress rehearsal, and then the show. Stevie was incredible that night—he played his ass off.

SHANNON That record tells the whole story of that gig. I don't think enough people have caught on to what a great performance he gave. That's some of my favorite playing from him, ever.

GW Through all of the success, had Stevie's personality or demeanor changed much?

SHANNON He was higher. We were all doing more drugs, and we were more fried from working so much.

GW As a band, though, it seemed that you had reached a new level of communication.

LAYTON I think we had. We were still having a hell of a lot of fun at that point, and the music was getting stronger.

SHANNON The band was still experiencing growth, and we kept the same basic integrity toward the music that we had from the beginning.

LAYTON We were basically healthy and excited. Success had taken hold. We were ridin' high. We felt like the fruits of our labors were just coming to bear. As far as the sound of the band, we were more fluid, the dynamics were more together, and we did feel tighter than ever.

GW During 1985, Stevie decided to bring in a second guitarist. What precipitated that decision?

SHANNON It was a spur-of-the-moment thing that eventually led to bringing Reese on board for *Soul to Soul*. Stevie invited [*guitarist*] Derek O'Brien and [*singer*] Angela Strehli to join us for a few weeks. It went over like a lead balloon! Stevie saw that it wasn't working, so he apologized and let them go.

LAYTON There were rhythm guitar parts on *Couldn't Stand the Weather* that could have been covered by another guitar player. Stevie thought, Derek can play these rhythm guitar parts, and I can concentrate on singing and soloing.

SHANNON I think he really wanted to get Derek and Angela some recognition. He wanted to show people that there were other great musicians from Austin. He loved both of them.

SOUL TO SOUL (1985)

GW Had you already started recording *Soul to Soul* when Reese came in?

LAYTON We'd been there for a couple of weeks. We'd cut "May I Have a Talk with You" [*released posthumously on* The Sky Is Crying] and a few other things. Joe Sublett hooked us up with Reese.

WYNANS I was playing with Joe in Delbert McClinton's band at the time. We had a gig in Dallas, where Stevie was recording, and Chris came over and brought us back to the studio.

LAYTON Stevie wanted keyboards for "Look at Little Sister," and that same night Joe recorded the sax solo on the tune. We knew Reese's playing from records he'd done with Delbert, Jerry Jeff Walker and Joe Ely, but none of us had ever even met him. Sublett said, "Reese is in Dallas tonight." I thought, Shit, it's his last night, and we're recording right down the street. Let's go meet him and see if he wants to come over.

GW Had you been discussing bringing in a keyboard player?

LAYTON Stevie thought we ought to add another member, because it would lend a new dimension, and maybe even a new direction, to the band.

SHANNON Now and again he would talk about adding keyboards and horns. The Carnegie Hall experience opened his eyes to new possibilities.

WYNANS The fact that they didn't know me led to the attitude of, "Well, let's bring him in and see what happens." They had already done takes of "Looking out the Window," "You'll Be Mine," "Empty Arms" and "Come On (Part III)." I added keyboards to these songs, and we recut the other songs, "Say What!" "Look at Little Sister," "Ain't Gone 'N' Give Up on Love," "Gone Home," "Change It" and "Life without You."

GW What was the origin of "Say What!"

SHANNON It was a jam, like Hendrix's "Rainy Day, Dream Away." We'd been doing that for a while. Stevie thought of breaking it down and singing, "Soul to soul!"

GW Was the wah-wah he used on "Say What!" one that had belonged to Jimi Hendrix?

LAYTON That's what I heard.

GW Doyle Bramhall, Sr. brought in a few tunes, didn't he? [*Singer/ songwriter/drummer Doyle Bramhall performed in bands with both Jimmie and Stevie Ray Vaughan in the late Sixties and early Seventies. In addition to influencing Stevie's vocal style, he wrote or co-wrote a number of songs for Stevie's albums and the Vaughan brothers'* Family Style *album (on which he also played drums)—Ed.*]

SHANNON Doyle brought in "Looking out the Window" and "Change It." We liked them both, and recorded them right away. "Look at Little Sister" is a song we'd been doing for a while. "Ain't Gone 'N' Give Up on Love" was a new tune that Stevie had just written. Reese came up with that great walk-up part on the bridge, which I thought was one of the coolest things about the song. "Gone Home" is by [*jazz sax great*] Eddie Harris. I'd heard Stevie play it on his own before. It's one of those songs that kind of faded into the record.

GW How did Stevie end up playing drums on "Empty Arms"?

SHANNON Stevie and I went in early one day and were jamming, with him on drums and me on bass. He was a great drummer, if he could last through the song! He said, "Let's do 'Empty Arms' real slow!" Richard [*Mullen*] didn't want to turn the tape machine on. Stevie said, "Turn it on!" and Richard's going, "What for?" [*laughs*] They got into an argument. Richard turned it on, and that's the one we kept. Stevie knew exactly what he had in mind on that tune. It ended up getting Vari-speeded up a few notches.

GW How did "Life without You" come together?

SHANNON That was a real personal song for Stevie. It was about Charley Wirz [*Wirz owned a guitar store in Dallas called Charley's Guitar Shop, and he built and repaired guitars for Vaughan—Ed.*], with whom Stevie was very close. He had died. Later on, it became Stevie's anthem: we'd break it down, and he'd talk about getting clean and sober, and about how he himself had almost died. [*to Reese*] Were you there when he recorded his vocals at Riverside?

WYNANS Yeah, I was.

SHANNON He was so scared, and I couldn't figure out why. He said, "This song means so much to me, and I'm afraid I won't be able to do it right."

GW That song has always struck me as Otis Redding's "(Sittin' on the) Dock of the Bay" meets Hendrix's "Bold as Love."

SHANNON Yeah, I agree. For the solo, I said, "Stevie, it would sound cool if you did something like the 'Bold as Love' solo," with that slow whine in the beginning.

WYNANS When we got to the solo part, we could all breathe and relax, and he just let go. That song, more so than any other, grew from a simple little tune into a giant anthem.

GW Reese, as a new person coming into the existing situation, how did the affairs of the band—in particular, the massive drug use—strike you?

WYNANS It was real chaotic. I figured I better get in there and get these guys shaped up! [*laughs*] If you spend too much time in the studio, you get this "burn-out" thing happening, where nothing sounds right, no matter what you do. The sound of the keyboards inspired Stevie, and it elevated his playing. The impression I got was that Tommy and Chris were really waiting for Stevie to get motivated. The drug use wasn't particularly alarming, because it was nothing I hadn't seen before.

GW Was Stevie happy with the finished product?

LAYTON He was, at least, relieved.

LIVE ALIVE (1986)

GW The next record, *Live Alive*, was wrought with problems. In later years, Stevie would say, "I didn't realize how bad a shape I was in at the time. There are more fix-it jobs on that record than I would have liked." The recordings are from the Montreux Jazz Festival of 1985, and shows in Austin and Dallas in July 1986.

SHANNON Stevie wanted to do a live record, because people had been asking for one for years. We also didn't have a lot of new material at the time, so it was an easy way to deliver a new album. Or, I should say, we thought it would be easy! [*laughs*]

LAYTON Doing a live record then was, like, "Help!" And it turned out to be the toughest live record to make, ever.

WYNANS We set up two or three shows at the Austin Opera House, and Stevie came up with a whole concept of what he wanted to do over there.

SHANNON There were sound problems, so we started to try to fix it up. And there begins the saga. In the process of fixing it, Stevie got creative and ended up getting too carried away, trying to do too much with it.

GW As these were live recordings, wasn't there a lot of "bleed" between all of the tracks?

LAYTON [*hysterical laughter*] Yes!

SHANNON That's what made it a nightmare.

LAYTON There were problems with the drum tracks—they sounded horrible. We were out at Stevie Wonder's studio [*Wonderland*] in L.A., and I tried to overdub new drum tracks. It sounded like fucking horseshit.

Some time after *Live Alive* was released, we were being interviewed, and I said, "Oh, that record was horrible!" Stevie shot me a look and said, "Hey, man!"

GW In the fall of 1986, you did a European tour of Denmark, Germany, Holland, France and Belgium. The Paris Olympia shows on September 23 and 24 revealed some serious problems.

SHANNON That was at the very end of our drugged-out period, when we'd really reached bottom. One of those nights, we played "Tin Pan Alley" for like 15 minutes.

LAYTON And Reese got so pissed off, he walked off the stage.

SHANNON Stevie got stuck in the wrong key, and just kept playing. I was thinking, God, that is not like Stevie at all. People in the audience got pissed off.

GW Four days later in Germany, Stevie became very ill.

LAYTON We were at the hotel, and Stevie wanted to get a drink. He and I went out together, but it was a late Sunday night, and everything was closed. He wasn't feeling good.

He said, "Goddamn, I need a fucking drink." I said, "No, you don't need a drink," because he was feeling sick to his stomach. Then, he began to throw up blood. Even after that happened, he kept saying he needed a drink. I told him he shouldn't, and he yelled at me: "I don't need a fucking drink, goddamn it, but I need a fucking drink!" I said, "Man, let's go back to the hotel." We went back to the hotel, and he laid in his bed. I called Tommy.

SHANNON He was laying on the bed, and he tried to get up, but couldn't. He threw up all over his chest, and it was a big puddle of blood.

LAYTON We called an ambulance, and these German medics showed up in long white coats, shouting German to one another. They pulled out I.V.s, and we were screaming, "Hey! Wait a minute! What the hell's going on?" They spoke not a word of English, and we spoke no German. They put I.V.s in him, and they wanted to take him to the hospital. We were yelling, "Where are you taking him? What's happening? How will we find him?"

They were giving him saline solution, because they'd determined, by looking at his eyes and checking his vital signs, that he was suffering from near-death dehydration. They were trying to hydrate him. While he was laying on the bed, I looked into his eyes, and it was like looking into the eyes of a dead deer, laying on the side of the road. They were almost dry, with no life in them. I got scared shitless.

SHANNON He started shaking, trembling, sweating.

LAYTON All of a sudden, the life came back into his eyes, and he said, "I need help," real weakly. I took that as the moment where he realized, this has got to change. Not like, "I need to get better so I can go back to doing what I've been doing," but "everything has to change."

GW Was there a gig scheduled for that night?

LAYTON No, but there was a gig the next night, in Zurich. After spending the night in the hospital, the next day we went to Zurich. That's where he made all of the phone calls; he called management, and that's when we began discussing taking Stevie to Dr. Victor Bloom, who had helped Eric Clapton and Pete Townshend get sober. We set up an appointment with Bloom, and after Zurich, we headed to London, for two scheduled shows. There were two or three days off before those London shows.

At that Zurich gig, I never heard Stevie sound so weak. He was drained. During the days off, he saw Dr. Bloom, and was visited by Eric Clapton. Then we did the London shows, at the Hammersmith Palais [*October 2*].

The headlines in the English press said "Vaughan Collapses on London Stage" and "Vaughan Falls Off Stage," but that was a lie. There was a gangplank, like you'd load a moving van with. The show was over and, before the encore, we all turned to walk off. This thing led off the stage to a doorway to the backstage area. Right as he got to the plank, they shut all the lights off, and we couldn't see a thing. In total darkness, he tried to step on it, and he stepped off the edge. He fell off the side and scraped his leg up. He said, "Fuck, man, I've had enough!"

"Stevie was real worried about playing after he'd gotten sober. He'd never really been sober, not since he was much younger. **He didn't know if he had anything left to offer.**"

—*REESE WYNANS*

The rest of the tour, which consisted of a bunch of Scandinavian dates, was cancelled. After that, Stevie flew to Atlanta and checked into the Charter Lane Rehabilitation Center, and Tommy went into rehab, too.

GW Once Stevie was in treatment, how would you describe his attitude?

SHANNON He felt real gung-ho about it, just as I did. We didn't know shit about what it was going to be like, to be honest. It was all brand-new, and we'd made it over 24 hours without a drink or drug. We knew that it was the right thing to do; it was the only thing we could do.

WYNANS Stevie was real worried about playing after he'd gotten sober. He'd never really been sober, not since he was much younger. He didn't know if he had anything left to offer.

SHANNON He wondered if he had "lost" it.

WYNANS Once we got back out on the road, he was very inspired and motivated. The shows became more cohesive and more energized; we had a "rock" show and a "blues" show, and the live shows gained momentum. There were great performances, and he proved that, yes, he still had plenty to say. Musically, everything got better and better.

IN STEP (1989)

GW Was Stevie a different kind of bandleader by the time he recorded *In Step*?

WYNANS Yes, in a lot of ways. He was real interested in working hard on the new material. We'd get together in the warehouse, and play and play and play. He also tried many different approaches to the songs, which is something he hadn't done before.

When we got back to the studio, instead of recording as we had with *Soul to Soul*—all of us in one room, making a huge wall of sound—his amps were isolated, so the sound wouldn't bleed into everything else. The drums, bass and keyboards were also recorded in a way so that we could get the best sound and the best performances. That method yielded a much better product.

LAYTON That was a cool period for the band. Stevie went off to write with Doyle [*Bramhall, Sr.*] in Dallas. He came back with "Wall of Denial," "The House Is Rockin' " and "Scratch-N-Sniff."

GW *In Step* featured the song "Crossfire," co-written by the three of you, along with Bill Carter and Ruth Ellsworth. This song became the only Number One hit Stevie ever had.

WYNANS Tommy had this riff [*the bass line, which is the song's primary riff*], and he wanted to write a soul tune. We put it together little by little, and it wasn't easy. We tried a whole bunch of different things with that song to make it work, and it came out just right.

SHANNON When Stevie first heard "Crossfire," it reminded him of "Shotgun," by Junior Walker.

GW He told me that, initially, he didn't know if it was a good song for him. He had to figure out where to play and where not to play, and he realized that it was okay to leave space for the band.

LAYTON Yeah, that's true. That was, in essence, a transformation for the band, and for him. It wasn't the kind of song that was based on the idea of, Let me come up with all of this guitar stuff, and y'all put your stuff underneath it. We had worked that way many times in the past, but this song required a different approach. And it was a success.

GW How did "The House Is Rockin' " come together?

WYNANS Stevie wanted to write a rock and roll song where the V [*five*] chord went on and on until it drove you crazy. So, that's what we did during the solo section. It's real simple; the chorus is just two chords—the I [*one*] and the V—back and forth.

GW Legendary rock guitar pioneer Paul Burlison, who is thanked in the liner notes, was supposed to come in and play on the record.

SHANNON He never made it. But Albert King did!

LAYTON Oh, gosh. This is so classic. He just showed up, and he ended up coming in several times. He kept picking on Stevie. He also asked Stevie if he could borrow some money. Stevie said, "How much do you need, Albert?" "About three thousand dollars." Stevie said, "Three thousand dollars? Well, okay."

Stevie loaned him the three thousand, and this was pretty early on in the making of the record. About the time we were getting ready to leave, Stevie said, "Hey, Albert, um...do you have that money?" And Albert says, "What money is that?" Stevie says, "That money that I loaned you." "That money you loaned me?" "Yeah," said Stevie, "I lent you three thousand dollars." And Albert goes, "Haw, haw haw! Now, come on, Stevie! You know you owe me!" [*laughs*]

GW "Tightrope," "Crossfire" and "Wall of Denial" are very confessional songs. Were there any discussions about how important the lyrical content was for him?

SHANNON "Tightrope" initially grew out of a jam between Whipper [*Chris Layton*], Reese and I. Stevie heard us jamming on that groove, and he put the song to the groove.

LAYTON We had come up with that "hopping funk" feel, and Stevie really dug it. A little while later, he came back with this song, and he said, "Play that groove again!"

SHANNON In terms of the lyrics, he was concerned about coming off as if he was preaching to people, which was something he really did not want to do. Now that he was clean and sober, it was the first time in his life he felt free to talk about what was going on in his life, and to sing and write about it, too. That is another way in which the music took a big turn: he wanted to put across a positive message to people.

LAYTON "Tightrope" and "Wall of Denial" turned out to be great songs, lyrically speaking. They are both about things that are really important, which made it cool for us. Content-wise, *In Step* became a real different kind of record compared to what we'd done in the past.

He was very concerned with self-analysis: how creative was he, and what did he have to give now that he was sober? He had questions about this, and he was a little afraid. We'd go into the studio at 11 A.M. or noon, and we might not hit a lick until six or seven in the evening, because he spent so much time getting guitar sounds. I couldn't help but wonder if a lot of that was him...

SHANNON Avoiding the inevitable.

LAYTON Yeah, getting up the nerve to get in there and say, "This is what I'm about."

SHANNON From my eyes, he went in scared to death. Song by song, you'd see him gain confidence. *In Step* was, for him, a big growing experience. In my opinion, it's our best studio album, and I think he felt that way, too. When we were done, he was very happy with the record, and the fact that he'd done it clean and sober. Finally, he could relax with the knowledge that he did have something to say. That record opened the door into the next phase of his life as a musician.

LAYTON That's true. On the last night I ever spoke with him, in Alpine Valley, I was struck by the confidence he had, and his excitement about the future, and how much he was looking toward our next record. It all started with *In Step*. By the time we had that conversation, his attitude was, "I'm here, I'm ready and I'm excited."

GW One of the standout tracks from *In Step* is "Riviera Paradise."

WYNANS Stevie looked at that song as a movie soundtrack, as a beautiful, soulful tune that could be thought of as backing up some touching love story.

SHANNON That was also one of those "first-take" songs.

LAYTON In fact, we were in the studio, and we had just done something real "up," like "Scratch-N-Sniff." Stevie said, "There's something I need to do. I want to record 'Riviera Paradise' because I need to make amends. This is the time. Let's turn the lights off."

We turned off all of the lights—we were in total darkness! I couldn't see him, or anyone else! The engineers weren't even ready for the take, because the cue-mix in the headphones was all wrong. He began to play just as they started the tape. It was really an instinct thing, because the arrangement hadn't even been discussed. When the song ended, there was just enough tape left on the reel to catch the natural fade of the instruments.

GW Jim Gaines has said that he was flipping out, trying to get your attention to bring the song to a close.

LAYTON Right. But because Stevie had turned all of the lights off, we were sitting there in darkness and couldn't see.

GW Stevie described "Riviera Paradise" as "praying through the guitar."

SHANNON This goes back to what we were talking about earlier: Stevie always played what he was feeling inside, as opposed to "with feeling." There is a big difference. Whatever was going on in his life, he'd express it through his guitar.

THE AFTERMATH

GW Ten years after Stevie's death, how would you assess his contributions to music?

LAYTON His influence is more vast than I ever imagined it could be. I hear it everywhere. With Stevie, we made records that were in the right spirit; they always rang true. We still carry that spirit with us today.

SHANNON For a long time, I heard many guitar players trying to get his tone. Eventually, the tone that all guitar players use had changed; what's considered a good tone these days has everything to do with Stevie. This is true even for some of the young players who may never have even listened to Stevie. In a subtle way, he has influenced them indirectly, and it's great to see.

WYNANS The most obvious thing to me is what's missing by his absence. No one has the phrasing and the style that Stevie had. While he was alive, Stevie represented the vanguard of blues music's popularity. Since his death, the popularity of blues has waned.

GW Stevie's music crossed over to a rock audience more successfully than any other blues musician.

SHANNON Stevie brought blues and rock together more successfully than anyone, next to and right along with Jimi Hendrix. When we would play "Texas Flood," the fans in the audience weren't thinking, Oh, this is blues. It was just a sound that they loved. Stevie took the blues and stretched it way past boundaries it had never crossed before.

WYNANS Stevie's music spoke very clearly and directly to so many. I think his catalog will remain a lasting tribute to him. And what he went through in his personal life inspired many, many people, and will continue to do so.

[8]

"When I heard the blues, it *killed* me,
it *slayed* me!"
—*STEVIE RAY VAUGHAN*

STEVIE RAY VAUGHAN:
THE LOST
INTERVIEWS

On three separate occasions between December 1986 and July 1989, *Guitar World* senior editor Andy Aledort spoke with Stevie Ray Vaughan about his metamorphosis into a blues guitar giant. These revealing conversations are presented here in their entirety.

BY ANDY ALEDORT

HIS **INTERVIEW TOOK PLACE** on December 2, 1986, shortly before Stevie Ray's performance at the Mid-Hudson Civic Center in downtown Poughkeepsie, New York. When I arrived at the venue, I was unaware that Stevie has just recently survived a near-death experience; the severe drug and alcohol addiction he was battling was still kept under wraps. It had been about six weeks since he'd left the London rehabilitation clinic of Dr. Victor Bloom (who had previously helped Stevie's friend Eric Clapton quit drinking), after which he checked into the Charter Peachford Hospital, in Atlanta, for a three-and-a-half-week stay. The Poughkeepsie performance was just Vaughan's eighth show sober.

Understandably to me now—but confusing to me then—the backstage vibe was very tense. Stevie's road manager was barking orders at everyone. But when I finally sat down with Stevie, he was in good spirits, though his energy level was curiously low. He was quiet, thoughtful and, at times, startlingly candid. We did, however, begin with a little 10-minute jam on a mid-tempo shuffle—just him and me through a small practice amp. It's a moment I'll never forget.

STEVIE RAY VAUGHAN It's one of those days, the sleepy kind. It's *cold* outside.

GUITAR WORLD How was your gig at Radio City Music Hall the other night?

VAUGHAN Oh, it was fine. It was fun. Most of our equipment is falling apart. [*Stevie plugs in his main guitar, Number One, and starts playing.*] Ooh, I'm outta tune!

GW What year is that guitar?

VAUGHAN '59.

GW How long have you had it?

VAUGHAN I've had it for 13 years. I bought it in about '73, I guess.

GW Did it look like that when you got it, or did the previous owner treat it better than you do?

VAUGHAN I don't treat it bad. It's just been around.

GW How did you first get started in music?

VAUGHAN When I was real young, [*country & western swing legends*] the Texas Playboys hung out at our house all the time. My parents played "42," and they'd come over and get drunk.

GW What's "42"?

VAUGHAN Dominoes. "42 to 84." Those guys hung around a lot. They'd do some playing and we'd hear their stuff. Mainly we'd hear them talking about it. There were a lot of "characters" hanging around.

GW Were [*Texas Playboy guitarists*] Eldon Shamblin or Junior Barnard among the guys who'd come over?

VAUGHAN Oh, God, I don't remember their names. I was a little beefheart. [*laughs*] Every once in a while my dad would yell [*in heavy Texas accent*], "Hey, Jim [*Stevie's older brother Jimmie*], Steve, come out here and show them what you can do!" And we were little midgets, with guitars hangin' on us that were this big!

GW How old were you when you first picked up the guitar?

VAUGHAN Seven. The first guitar I had was one of those Roy Rogers guitars; it had pictures of cowboys and cows on it, some rope. I had a blanket that had the same shit on it, too.

"The first guitar I had was **one of those Roy Rogers guitars.**"

GW Did you sleep with the guitar and the blanket together?

VAUGHAN Yeah! [*laughs*] I *still* sleep with my guitar, when my woman ain't around!

GW Do you remember the first records that you listened to?

VAUGHAN Jimmie turned me on to a lot of different stuff. I remember several different things: I remember him bringing home Hendrix, Buddy Guy, Muddy Waters, B.B. King.

The first record I ever bought was "Wham" by Lonnie Mack, from 1963. I'm glad it wasn't the Monkees. [*laughs*] "Wham" was a great record. I played it so many times, my dad broke it! He got mad and broke it because I played it over and over and over and over. When I didn't think it could be any louder, I went and borrowed somebody's Shure Vocal Master P.A., put mikes in front of the stereo speakers and then turned the P.A. up. It was *loud* in my room.

GW And there went your records.

VAUGHAN Not long after that. Every time he broke it, I just went and got another one.

GW What did you pick up from listening to Lonnie Mack?

VAUGHAN A lot of inspiration, I can tell you that. Between listening to that guy's *feeling* in his music and watching my brother and how much feeling he had with it, I mainly just picked up big-time inspiration. What I was getting out of it wasn't so much technical or anything; just the thought of them playing made me want to jump up and play.

GW The spirit of it is what affected you the most?

VAUGHAN Yeah.

GW What bands was Jimmie playing in back in those days?

VAUGHAN He had several bands, such as the Swingin' Pendulums, and he was with Sammy Laurie and the Penetrations. You know the song "Penetration"? It was pretty cool. I can't remember how it went. I'm a little cleaner nowadays than I was for a few years. My memory kind of went *pffft!*

[*Guitarist*] Johnny Peoples was on "Penetration," too. He played in the Chessmen with Jimmie.

GW What kind of music did these bands play?

VAUGHAN It was rock and roll, rhythm and blues. He was always interested in all of that stuff. In the Penetrations, they did Sammy Laurie tunes. Obviously, they were into girls. [*laughs*]

GW As in, penetrate your pants?

VAUGHAN [*laughing so hard, he spits his coffee all over his pants*] Oh, shit! God damn! I'll be right back! [*He leaves to get cleaned up, and then returns.*]

GW How did you end up playing drums on "Empty Arms," from *Soul to Soul*?

VAUGHAN I wanted to.

GW You said, "It's my record, so I'm playing drums"?

VAUGHAN No. [*laughs*] Me and the bass player [*Tommy Shannon*] were in the studio by ourselves, and he and I like to play bass and drums together. We were just messin' around. When we started it off, that song was real slow—slow enough where it's hard to keep going at the same speed. Then we sped it up 13-1/2 percent with the Varispeed and recorded the rest of the song to it. When we laid it down, it was like [*sings very slowly*], "DA...da DA...da DA..." Try to keep that tempo going without speeding up or slowing down. It's hard.

"I still listen to Hendrix, all the time. I doubt I'll ever quit."

GW Besides Lonnie Mack, what were some of the other records you first played along with?

VAUGHAN [*The Yardbirds'*] "Jeff's Boogie," of course. "Over Under Sideways Down."

GW "Happenings Ten Years Time Ago" and "Psycho Daisies"?

VAUGHAN Yeah. Lots of Hendrix, of course. Clapton's stuff with Mayall. Get your Rickenbacker bass and go crazy playing "Lady Madonna," just like everybody. Did you do that too?

GW Yeah. The bass part was the whole song.

VAUGHAN How many hours did you spend on it?

GW Not enough.

VAUGHAN I got it right a couple of times, and then I'd start it over and screw it up.

GW Did you listen to much T-Bone Walker?

VAUGHAN Yeah. "T-Bone Shuffle," "Stormy Monday," "Cold, Cold Feeling." A lot of 'em I don't remember the names of; I just know the way they go. I had a bunch of his records.

GW Were you listening to T-Bone before you heard Hendrix?

VAUGHAN No, it was after, mostly. I listened to Hendrix first. See, I still listen to Hendrix, all the time. I doubt I'll ever quit.

T-Bone was the first guy to play behind his head, and on his back, on the floor. Those were all T-Bone tricks. And Guitar Slim.

GW Did you listen to jazz guitarists, like Kenny Burrell or Wes Montgomery?

VAUGHAN Yeah, Kenny Burrell.

GW "Gone Home," from *Soul to Soul*, is in that West Coast, Kenny Burrell style.

VAUGHAN Yes, it is. We play "Chitlins Con Carne" by Kenny Burrell. [*lets out a huge yawn*] You'll have to excuse me today; I'm asleep. I haven't been stoned in a long time; I'm straight now. This is me *straight*, believe it or not. [*laughs*] It's 51 days today since I had a drink.

GW How come?

VAUGHAN 'Cause I want to.

GW How do you feel?

VAUGHAN Lots better. Kinda crazy today, but I'm okay.

GW What other jazz guitar players did you listen to?

VAUGHAN Wes Montgomery. Django Reinhardt. Grant Green. He's got some *tone*, man. Jackie King. Fred Walters. The Wes stuff is his recordings with trios and quartets. My favorite Wes record, for some reason, had an orchestra on it; it's called *In the Wee Small Hours*. Sometimes it sounds like Muzak, but what he played on it...Kenny Burrell played rhythm guitar on it.

GW Are there specific guitar things that you picked up from Wes?

VAUGHAN Every once in a while, something just comes out. I can't read music; I can't read a note. But every once in a while, I feel the "Wes" thing coming. I can't do it just sitting here. I've got to be groovin' out.

JUNE 23, 1989
NEW YORK OFFICES OF EPIC RECORDS

THIS INTERVIEW TOOK place shortly before Stevie Ray's *In Step* album was to be released. Songs like "Crossfire," "Tightrope" and "Riviera Paradise" had yet to receive radio airplay, so Stevie and I were able to speak about them without the influence of knowing just how successful these songs would soon be. Stevie began by autographing a stack of pictures a photographer friend of mine had taken at the Poughkeepsie show, and then picked up my guitar and continued to play it throughout the interview. The well-kept secret of his drug rehabilitation was now something he wanted to share with the world, in the hope of helping even just one person in a similar predicament. He wasted no time getting to what was foremost on his mind.

"The biggest problem I had was self-centeredness and ego. That's really what addiction seems to boil down to."

GUITAR WORLD How long has it been since you recorded the last studio album, *Soul to Soul*?

STEVIE RAY VAUGHAN Four years. We cut *Soul to Soul* in May of '85.

GW Why the delay?

VAUGHAN I guess the world had to turn around a few times, and so did I.

GW Since emerging from drug rehabilitation, how has playing music changed for you?

VAUGHAN The hardest thing to deal with isn't what I thought it would be. I thought the hardest thing would be, "Oh God, now I'm straight—can I still play?" That had nothing to do with it. The hardest part is trying to keep things in perspective. I found out that the biggest problem I had was self-centeredness and ego. That's really what addiction seems to boil down to. To keep that part of yourself under control while everybody's telling you how great you are is quite a task.

GW Is it difficult to see what's really going on without being swayed by what people tell you?

VAUGHAN Yeah. Finding some kind of perspective is the hardest part, because I want to stay alive and I want to stay as healthy as possible, and grow in that way. It is getting a lot easier, in some ways. However, every time I think I've learned something, I realize that I've just uncovered a big hole! [*laughs*] A big empty spot, or one that's going, "Arrrggghhh!"

GW Being a blues musician is about expressing your feelings, and communicating those feelings to the audience. How has the emotional upheaval you've experienced affected you as a musician?

VAUGHAN One thing I've noticed is that songs I used to sing *at* people I should have been singing at myself. At least I think that way.

GW Do you hear the words more now?

VAUGHAN Oh, God, yeah. Different songs mean different things than I used to think they meant, too. To put it mildly, a lot of blues tunes have to do with resentments, big time. [*laughs*] Take "Cold Shot." I used to sing that at certain women that I've been involved with over the years. Even though I didn't write it, I had in my head the way I related to it. Since I sobered up, I realized that *I* left; *I* was the one who gave the cold shot. And it hurts when you realize that you've hurt somebody, as opposed to, all this time, you've been telling yourself how bad they'd hurt you. Those words could really be telling me that I hurt myself. There are also other songs that are *kinder* than I thought. They make me feel better than I knew.

GW What are you finding there that makes it feel so good?

VAUGHAN A whole new world. A whole new chance for myself. I find that, more than ever, if I don't play the best I possibly can, and really try to play better than I think I can, then I've wasted my chance. 'Cause I'm playing on borrowed time. Left to my own devices, I would have killed myself, however slowly. Now I have a new chance. My best thinking just about killed me, okay? It just so happens that I'm not dead! [*laughs*] Somebody else helped me to stay alive. I just allowed it to happen.

GW I think those feelings translate to the music on the new album. How did you get that elusive quality on record?

VAUGHAN Most of the time, the whole band played together live. It was kind of a difficult record to make. We had fun, but we started and stopped a lot of times because of amp problems I was having. There were amps that I had to send back and forth to California to get worked on because we couldn't get a hold of the right schematics for them.

GW Was that the old Vibroverbs and Super Reverbs?

VAUGHAN No. We had someone there to work on the Fenders and the Marshalls. I had to go through a lot of speakers to find some that I really liked, and we ended up *spraying* every amp with these speakers.

GW What became of the amps you used on *Soul to Soul*?

VAUGHAN They weren't holding up. For some reason, in the room we were in, a lot of things sounded darker, tonewise. We were in Kiva Studios [*in Memphis*], and the rooms were all wood. I was having a hard time getting amps to hold up: I'd turn 'em on, set 'em to a real good sound and turn 'em off to let 'em cool down. When it was time to play, I'd turn 'em back on, and one of 'em would die. It would either start going "*ackhhkhk*" or "*bllpppp*" or blow up, or something cool. [*laughs*] I'd hit a couple of notes and it would start making bad, horrible noises. The setup changed from day to day. The amps were dying like flies. This sounds crazy, but I took 32 amps with me. I figured, if worse came to worse, there would always be something I could pull out of a road case. I'm glad I took so many amps, because we ended up having only about three or four that worked. In fact, I bought an old '59 Fender Bassman and used the same settings for the whole session. I loved it! It was the one amp that stayed right the whole time. All these new-fangled custom amps I had kept falling apart.

GW Did you end up using a combination of Marshalls, Dumbles and Vibroverbs?

VAUGHAN You almost pegged it. Usually, I had one Dumble, one Marshall, the Bassman and a Super Reverb. I ran them all at the same time, but they were miked differently and set differently. Sometimes, I ran the effects through them. When I say effects, I'm talking about a Fuzz Face, a Tube Screamer or a wah-wah pedal. I also had a Leslie in another room.

The weirdest part of it was that we had to build this thing that looked like a square baseball backstop, made out of chicken wire. There was either a radio station or some kind of microwave stuff that came through the studio. You'd be playing along, and all of a sudden there'd be these weird clicks and buzzes coming out of the amps. But if I stood inside this *cage* that they made [*laughs*], it wouldn't happen. They caged me!

The record took a while to make because of the amp problems, and also because, when I write songs, sometimes they have to grow for a while. We can rehearse, rehearse, rehearse, and it just sounds like we chopped, chopped, chopped.

GW Are all the originals new tunes?

VAUGHAN "Travis Walk" we've been doing for about three months. "Riviera Paradise" I wrote about four or five years ago. "Love Me Darlin' " I've been doing since I was about three, [*laughs*] or at least 10 years. "Wall of Denial" we played in the warehouse; that was the only time. I never learned exactly how to sing it before we did it for the record. "Tightrope" we'd done at two gigs. "Scratch-N-Sniff" we tried to do at one or two gigs. "The House Is Rockin' " we'd done at two gigs. Most of it was new stuff.

GW "Tightrope" features some great interplay between you and Chris Layton, especially at the end of your first solo. Was it difficult to get that in the studio?

VAUGHAN We got an idea of how we wanted it to go. That was one of the songs that I only played rhythm on when we first cut it. I didn't like the tone I had when I was putting down the rhythm track, so when it came up to the solo, I decided just to groove! It wasn't intentional. [*laughs*] Then, I went back and played the whole song again with the old track a little bit in one side of the headphones, and I played the solo where I was supposed to the first time. We ended up using both tracks together. That's how we overdub—we just do it by saying, "Okay, roll the tape!"

GW So there isn't a rhythm guitar track behind most of the solos on the other songs?

VAUGHAN No. The only other song that has one is "Scratch-N-Sniff."

GW Did you record the rhythm track first, and then the solo?

VAUGHAN Yeah. I was thinking about getting [*legendary rockabilly guitarist*] Paul Burlison to play on the record, but he never came back into town! We'd talked about it a little bit, but it never happened. He was telling us about how he got the sounds on the old records: he dropped his amp. [*laughs*] Broke a tube. That was it. But he never came back, so he's not on the record.

When I was doing the "Scratch-N-Sniff" solo, I hated everything I played. I went, "Hmm, let me try this one more time," and I turned on all the gadgets I had, including the wah, and started playing this. [*hits a big high note with lots of vibrato*]

GW *In Step* has a lot of the funky rhythm guitar parts that you always played live but never put on an album. On "Tightrope," as soon as you start doing it, you get into some great rhythmic interplay with Chris.

VAUGHAN The Whipper. That stuff seems to be the freshest when we first start doing it, but, if we're not careful, those things turn into crutches, in a way. Like the automatic "kicks" that people can get stuck on.

"Tightrope" and "Wall of Denial" are a lot different, musically, but lyrically they're almost the same song—just different phases of it.

GW Stevie Wonder is someone who has been able to write great music that also carries a message, which is hard to do. I think you've done it very successfully with the songs on this record. The last thing you'd want to do is to sound "preachy."

VAUGHAN No, I really don't want that. It's real important to me to write about that stuff. I spent so long with this image of, "I'm cooler than so and so because I get higher than he does." And I really believed it for a long time. But it's just not true.

GW Life doesn't have to be an Iron Man contest.

VAUGHAN No, it doesn't! [*laughs*] And I'd just as soon spend the rest of these years making it clear that it's not true.

GW Was it hard to get these feelings down in a song?

VAUGHAN I went back and forth between feeling really strongly about it and wondering if anybody really wants to hear this shit or not. I knew that I meant it, that I felt good about it sometimes. I was afraid that I'd turn people off. Somewhere along the line, that stopped mattering, because if they got turned off, it'd only be for a time. I've been there before, when somebody would try to tell me that I had a problem. I'd go, [*growling*] "Of course I do! Goddamn it, don't you think I know that?" I just had to come to grips with it.

GW It's an ambitious endeavor to write something purely from the heart in that way. It's something that some of your favorite musicians, like Stevie Wonder and Jimi Hendrix, have been able to do in their music.

VAUGHAN What's amazing to me about a lot of Hendrix's stuff is what he was talking about, especially toward the end of his life. He wasn't talking about "Let's party." He wasn't at all.

GW "Crash Landing" is in that category, but it really hasn't gotten its due.

VAUGHAN And "Angel." People come up to me and say, "Oh, I knew Hendrix, and you have to remember that he was on acid all the time, and he was just rhyming." Yeah, *right*. He did a lot musically and lyrically. Tonewise, look how much difference he made. I don't think anybody's stretched tone past there yet. And he came up with it!

GW How did you develop your soloing style?

VAUGHAN It's a real weird mixture. It's kind of everything from my generation to Muddy Waters at the same time. It goes back to my brother Jimmie, when he was bringing home all these different records. It might have been because I was a little kid, but it seemed like, all at the same time, he brought home the Bluesbreakers with Eric Clapton, Howlin' Wolf, B.B. King, Muddy Waters and the Beatles. It was like, "Here comes Jimmie with the record world!" [*laughs*]

GW The whole history of recorded music was under his arm.

VAUGHAN Yeah! And he knew what he was doing. At the same time, my parents had these friends, and their son came over with his guitar and showed us how to play stuff by Jimmy Reed and Ray Sharpe and the Razorblades. So all of that was going on, and then somewhere not far down the line, Jimmie brings home this Jimi Hendrix record, and we both went, "Ahhh! What's this?"

GW Was it *Are You Experienced*?

VAUGHAN That, and a 45. I'm a little confused about which one. So all at the same time, there were these different influences. By the time I was 12, Jimmie was gone. Here he was, the hottest guitar player I knew of, and he was considered the hottest guitar player in Texas at age 15. I think he started playing when he was 12. [*laughs*]

GW Wasn't he called "Freddie King, Jr." when he was 15?

VAUGHAN Yeah, he was. I mean, what do you do but get excited when all this is going on? If you want to know what made me go crazy with it, it was watching him. Not trying to out-do Jimmie, but, shit, what do you do but pick up the ball and run? It's not trying to pass him, and it's not trying to keep up with him. It's more like, Wow! Look what big brother stumbled onto! A lot of people seem to think that we're trying to beat each other at something, but it's not that at all. I saw him get real exciting—not just excited, but *exciting*—with something, and that excited me. I didn't know what else to do.

GW What were some of the slow blues that you listened to that helped you in developing your style?

VAUGHAN Albert King records, for one thing. B.B. King's *Live at the Regal*, Albert King's *Born Under a Bad Sign*, it was called first, or *King of the Blues Guitar*. Believe it or not, I remember seeing Albert King on TV doing "Born Under a Bad Sign," and I was like, "Yes!"

GW Do you remember when he did the Miller Beer commercial?

VAUGHAN No!

GW It was around '72 or '73. They played it during New York Knicks games. He'd say, "Hey, waiter, bring me a Miller...please?" and "That's my Miller, get your hands off that!"

VAUGHAN [*laughs*] Oh, man, I never saw that!

GW Hendrix was obviously a big Albert King fan, and I think it's interesting how your style assimilates portions of both. When Hendrix played Albert licks, he still sounded more like himself than like Albert.

VAUGHAN I'm glad that Hendrix sounded like Hendrix when he played. [*laughs*] And I think he was glad he sounded like himself, too.

GW Was Johnny Winter ever an influence on you?

VAUGHAN Yes, in different ways. Mostly later. I just didn't hear him that much early on. I listened to him after I knew Tommy [*Shannon*].

GW You were 14 when you met Tommy?

VAUGHAN Yeah, and we started playing together not long after that. For some reason, I didn't hear Johnny Winter that much, and I don't even know why. Part of it was that I wasn't listening to the radio that much. I was just stuck off in my own little world. When I did listen to the radio, it was a little crystal set, and I listened to Ernie's

Record Mart. With a crystal radio! I'd lay there at night and listen to all these blues specials, and they'd advertise 38-record sets! [*laughs*] They played stuff that I don't even think was available anywhere else except through these Record Mart deals. They had things like Little Milton, B.B. King, Albert King, Jimmy Reed and on and on. There wasn't very many of us white guys on it.

GW In your opinion, what is it about the blues that makes it such a vital and powerful form of music?

VAUGHAN It just sounds more like "the real thing" than anything else. It's not like I automatically said, "This is cooler than this" or "This has more emotion." When I heard it, it *killed* me, it *slayed* me! There was just not a question. Hearing it all these different ways, from the English Blues Boom to authorized recordings to shitty bootleg stuff of everybody you can dream of—it was like, if you can hear it, do it. It's funny, because I don't like that there are bootlegs of *me* out there, but I'm glad I got to hear everyone else's! From listening and listening and listening, the more I heard, the better I liked it.

GW Have your feelings for the blues changed over the years?

VAUGHAN I feel like I've gotten more in touch with the blues in recent years. I usually feel that way when I see somebody play who's used to playing clubs, and isn't used to running around in a fancy tour bus and playing arenas. There's a difference there. It's as if the record companies say, "The guy sounds that way, so we can't sell him." But then, after that guy has been successful, it's as if he says, "I've been sold, so I can't sound like that anymore." Every time I get to hear somebody sound *real*, I get the chance to come home, inside. That makes me want to play that way even that much more, so I can still snicker when someone says, "Hey, the record sold!" [*laughs*]

GW Can you hear that quality in your own playing when you listen back to your recordings?

VAUGHAN Sometimes, and it makes me feel good, because I know that I'm still alive.

GW The solo on "Wall of Denial" is one of your best; you're not holding back at all.

VAUGHAN I was jumping up and down! It was real important to us. We had fun on that, man. We had trouble with this and that on the record, but we had fun, too. I learn tricks every once in a while, and by tricks I mean ways to do things. For that solo, I used a Leslie [*rotary speaker cabinet*], but it was noisy on the slow speed. So I took a Variac [*a variable voltage transformer used to control the speed of an industrial-style motor—Ed.*], put it on the slow speed, and then put the Leslie on the fast speed, making the Leslie go a little faster than slow, without making any clunking noises as it went around.

GW Did you use Number One for most of *In Step*?

VAUGHAN No, just for some of it. I used the white Strat body with a Telecaster neck on some of it. I used the butterscotch one, which is a '61. On "Wall of Denial," I used Number One.

GW That guitar has such a unique sound. It's like a growl.

VAUGHAN I know. But I can't use it all the time because, for some reason, it wants to rattle real bad. The low E will be this high, and it still rattles. I had to change the neck; I took the neck off the butterscotch one and put it on Number One. I still have the original neck. For years, Rene [*Martinez, Vaughan's guitar tech*] had been taking the frets out, filling the fret slots in, and then putting new frets in. Over time, the slots got too big, mainly on the edges. I've been using big frets for so long, it only made it worse.

The neck has also been broken near the headstock. Have you ever seen Jimmie throw his guitar? I learned this trick from him, except his guitar never broke! [*laughs*] I was playing in Lubbock, back in '81, and when I threw it, it hit this paneled wall and the wood snapped. The guitar laid there on the ground: some of the strings went up, and some of them went down. It was making this *"blubgbbngbg!"* noise by itself, and I was standing there, going, "Yeah!" [*laughs*] It was during "Third Stone from the Sun," and it sounded fine, like it was supposed to be there. But then I cried later. That's another story there.

JULY 3, 1989

THIS INTERVIEW WAS conducted via phone, with Stevie Ray at his home in Texas. We continued to speak at length about the recording of *In Step*; at times during the interview, Stevie played musical examples through the same '59 Bassman amp he used on the album. After some time on the phone, he had to head over to the airport to pick up Chris Layton, so we continued the interview via his car phone as he rolled down the highway.

GUITAR WORLD As you mentioned previously, most of the basics for *In Step* were cut live in the studio. How did the band achieve such great interplay?

STEVIE RAY VAUGHAN We were able to watch each other pretty close. We were set up so that we could play live: Tommy had an iso [*isolation*] booth for his amp, but he was in the same room with Chris. Reese had an iso booth for his Leslie, and I had an iso booth for me *and* my rig. That way, I could get some response out of my rig, but I had a window so I could see in the control room on one side of the room, and see Chris on the other side of the room. And we'd watch each other. Also,

I had a talkback mic, so I could holler, whistle [*laughs*] or, if I could remember the words, sing the vocal part.

GW Was everyone wearing headphones?

VAUGHAN Yeah.

GW Do you find this setup to be the most comfortable way to record?

VAUGHAN Yeah. We tried to record without headphones, but the main problem is that I play loud.

GW How loud do you play in the studio as compared to a gig?

VAUGHAN Pretty much the same. In some cases, quieter, and in some cases, louder. Every room sounds different. I'm trying to learn some things about wood and the characteristics of the sound. Kiva Studios is a completely wooden room—finished wood—and if I wasn't real careful, I ended up having a sound that was too dark. In the studio, my Bassman was set so it sounded so crystalline, so clear and high-endy, but when I got it home, it sounded horrible! But in the studio, it sounded good.

Back to what we were talking about, as a rule, this way seemed to be an easier way to record. For one thing, we each had a little mixing board right next to us, so we could make our own headphone mixes. We were all able to watch each other, and that way we were playing to each other and with each other, so that it was real spontaneous. At the same time, there was good separation because of the iso booths, and the drums were in the big room to get the big sound. And Tommy was in there, too, feeling it with Chris. It worked out real well.

When we did *Soul to Soul*, we had every amp that I owned at the time hooked up. And they were all in the room with us. We also had a huge P.A. in there—it was some ungodly number of watts—with a 30-inch subwoofer that we used for monitors. [*laughs*] For amps, I had two Dumbles, a couple of Marshalls, a bunch of Fenders, and then it trailed off to the side. It was kind of like a galaxy of amps. It spread out like the Milky Way! We just had some foam rubber between my amps and the drums.

GW Did that result in a loss of separation?

VAUGHAN Yeah, it did. We had to go in and dissect things, and take some of the "bleed" out. There was less bleed than we thought there would be, but you can hear some ghost vocal on that record. The isolation we used for *In Step* worked better, and I was still next to my rig so I could get the response.

GW How big was the room you were standing in?

VAUGHAN About 25 by 15.

GW The whole studio must be pretty large, then.

VAUGHAN Oh, yeah.

GW Did you put a scratch vocal down every time?

VAUGHAN Not on every song, because I just wanted to concentrate on my playing. I did scratch vocals on "Leave My Girl Alone," "Let Me Love You" and "Crossfire." I killed the poor mikes I was singing in! I was singing as loud as I could, just trying to get all the feeling out of it.

GW Your singing sounds great on the record—very powerful. You sound like you're really putting out.

VAUGHAN I'm trying to. We took some time to do the vocals—could have taken a lot more time—but it was framed around other projects for the producer [*Jim Gaines*] and the engineers, and we had a gig in New Zealand to get to. It didn't seem like a good idea to try to back out of that. It was a benefit for Greenpeace that we wanted to do real bad.

GW How long did it take to record *In Step*?

VAUGHAN Fifteen weeks, start to finish. That's not counting the writing of the songs. We had a couple of breaks to do different things.

GW Were you expected to record the album faster than that?

VAUGHAN Eight to 10 was the original plan of some people involved, but I said that that was unrealistic.

GW How long did *Soul to Soul* take?

VAUGHAN About three months. That's a realistic amount of time. If we get it done faster, great, but I don't like to lock myself into six weeks, you know? Some people spend a real long time in the studio, and I wouldn't want to get stuck like that, either. You tend to take the songs apart, put 'em back together, and you end up sterilizing them. I've heard of people slaving together four or five 24-track machines, and you have 100 zillion tracks going at once. I don't see that as a solution, but I like to leave myself room so that I don't feel *too* pressured. At the same time, I don't want to feel like I don't have to do any work, because, given the space, I can be a procrastinator. I like a fixed amount of time, within reason. I like to work at a relaxed pace, but I do like to get back out on the road.

GW In what order did you record the songs on *In Step*?

VAUGHAN We did "Tightrope" and "Wall of Denial" in the first few days. And there were some songs that we recorded but ended up not using.

GW How many extra tunes were there?

VAUGHAN There were five more that we recorded, and there were two versions of one of them.

GW Were any of these Hendrix tunes?

VAUGHAN No, not this time. There are a lot that we'd like to record, but it was important to us that this record show where we come from, as much as possible. In fact, I was afraid there wasn't enough blues on it. As it turns out, we actually recorded a few more blues tunes that didn't make the record. We recorded a Sly Williams song, "Boot Hill" [*released posthumously on* The Sky Is Crying], and I play slide on the whole thing.

I used my Charlie Christian guitar for that, and it sounded *horrible*, but the right kind of horrible. [*laughs*] It was real fat. It sounded like it's supposed to. But, once again, we keep trying to do it in a key that's too high for me to sing. And I should know by now, because we've recorded that song for every record except *Texas Flood*. And we did it too high again. The track does sound real good, though. We'll do it again, in a lower key next time. I've got my Charlie Christian with me on the road now, tuned down to C♯ or C; I forget which one.

GW Is that the key you can sing it in?

VAUGHAN Yeah.

GW What kind of slide do you use?

VAUGHAN A Mighty Mite brass slide. I learned how to play slide with a Kraft Pimento Cheese jar and a baby food jar, worn on my middle and ring fingers together. After a while, I started using shot glasses, wine glasses, champagne glasses, beer glasses. [*laughs*] It got to be funny; I'd use whatever was around. Now, I'm used to playing with a real heavy metal slide. I try to get a real deep, big, huge, *old* sound.

GW "Crossfire" reminds me of some of the Albert King stuff that was recorded at Stax.

VAUGHAN Yeah. The first time I heard that song it reminded me a whole lot of Junior Walker. I thought it was a neat song, but it was arranged in a slightly different way, and I was uncomfortable playing it. I didn't know what to play. And it was hard to admit that I didn't know what to play. I just said, "This is weird!" [*laughs*]

GW It was the song's fault.

VAUGHAN Yeah. "This song's weird, man!" But then I came to grips with it. I had to let the band carry the riff, and it's taken me a while to learn to let the band carry what they're going to carry anyway, you know? I don't have to be all over everything to make it work.

There are songs I've never really finished writing. They're like babies that never grew up. They become stuff for the next record, and that feels good. It's funny, because I went through a grieving process when we were done tracking and these songs didn't make the record. It was like my babies never grew up! [*laughs*] So I just sat in my room and played them by myself.

GW It must be a great feeling when you build up a new song in the studio and hear it develop.

VAUGHAN It is, because some of it I can hear in my head, but I can't always convey it to somebody else. On one of the songs, I sat down at the drum throne and, while I played the guitar part, I played bass drum and hi-hat with my feet, and showed them where I wanted it. Then we tried the song, and it sounded real cool. But sometimes, instead of letting the song go where it was going, we'd try to change it up into something else, and we'd lose where I was coming from in the first place.

GW Did you record anything on the National Steel guitar that you're holding on the cover of the album?

VAUGHAN Not this time, but I had planned on it. I did record one song with the 12-string acoustic [*"Life By the Drop," released on* The Sky Is Crying]. It was just me. I recorded it that way because it sounded more personal. However, I did several takes, and the more we worked on it, the more the producer and myself heard it as a band song. I may go in and record it with the guy who wrote it, Doyle Bramhall—the father, not the son.

GW "Tightrope" has the lyric, "There was love all around me, but I was looking for revenge. Thank God it never found me, would have been the end."

VAUGHAN A lot of times, our fears keep us from seeing what's really there. I got a glimpse of what life would be like without my fears, without my guilt and my shame—without that club to beat myself over the head with. It was just for a couple of minutes. I never realized how much those feelings and those emotions permeate everything. I got a glimpse of how I felt without all of that, and I felt a lot better about everything and everybody. It was a real neat deal. I was just talking to somebody, and they said something that sparked it. It was like being in a completely smoke-filled room—like a cloud [*laughs*]—and then somebody turned on a vent and all the smoke was gone for a minute.

I learned all that stuff—the guilt and the shame—when I was a little kid. I learned how to be afraid all the time, because it wasn't very constant at home. I don't know if everybody else in the family perceived it the same way. Probably not. But I learned real quickly not to know what to expect, so therefore I'd just stay out of the way, and keep my feelings out of the way. If something bad happened, and I had feelings about it, then it must have been my fault. I didn't realize how deeply that was embedded in me. Without someone else doing it, I do it to myself, because I'm familiar with that, you know? It's a shame.

GW For whatever the reason, that stuff is self sustaining.

VAUGHAN Uh huh. I'm just now learning how to let go of some of that, and I can't always do it. Sometimes, I can put the club down. And other times, I pick it right back up and go to flogging myself. [*laughs*] It's an old pattern that I have to learn how not to do.

GW Do those feelings ever come out while you're playing?

VAUGHAN Sometimes they crawl all over me. It happened the other night: we're playing along, and all of a sudden I start feeling all of this self-conscious crap crawling all over me. You just want to tear your skin off and run!

GW It's like a vine crawling up your leg.

VAUGHAN Yeah, except, believe me, it's already all over my head! [*laughs*] And then I opened my eyes and I saw all these people watching us, really having a blast, and I thought, What am I *doing* to myself? These people accept us. I'm the only one who's not accepting myself right now.

There's something to always wanting to be better; it gives us a reason to try to grow. But it's not all right to allow myself to be unaccepting of everything. The audience was honestly enjoying what we were doing, and I was sabotaging it. It's an easy thing to do sometimes. But in reality, all I have to do is stop and look where I've come from. That has to do with how my life is changing for the better. If I stop and look at where I found myself before I got clean, where I'm at now is a little better than when I was puking up blood and bile in the middle of the street.

GW When I saw you at the Pier in New York last summer, there was this relentless intensity to your guitar playing. After your problems with drug addiction, I wondered if and how it would affect your playing. What I heard was a tremendous outpouring of good feelings.

VAUGHAN Well, I have to keep trying. And I do. I know that everything is better now, and I do mean *everything*. My whole life is better. It's hard for me to see that when everything is better, my music is too. There's no reason why it shouldn't be. I'm not saying that it's an automatic deal—I have to work at these things harder than ever. And that's fine with me. I'm glad I do. It has to do with progression, and there's healthy and unhealthy sides to it. The balance is the thing to find.

GW On *In Step*, are the slide ups at the beginning of "Love Me Darlin'" based on what Hubert Sumlin played on the original?

VAUGHAN Yeah. It's just more evident because I've got my Fuzz Face on, and I get more of a *ripping* sound. Hubert had a real crystal clear sound, almost too crystal clear to be true. I've always tried to figure out how in the hell he got that sound. I still haven't gotten it. I've gotten close, but he gets this *natural* sound.

GW How did the song "Travis Walk" come about?

VAUGHAN We were in a rehearsal hall, working on "Scratch-N-Sniff," and we couldn't decide what we wanted to do. We stopped for a minute; everybody was real frustrated. I walked over to the corner, looked at this picture of my brother and jumped into playing the tune! [*laughs*] He just looked so cool in the picture.

GW When you write, do you think at all about the style the tunes are in or where they're coming from?

VAUGHAN It's just a sound I hear in my head and a feeling I have. I don't know how to decipher between my thoughts and my feelings and, in a way, that's real good. It's confusing sometimes, when you're trying to weed through 'em. [*laughs*] But when I hear something, it makes me feel a certain way. And when I feel something, often I'll hear certain things. Then, I try to act on it in a constructive way, which is to *play*.

GW On this record, particularly on "Tightrope," "Crossfire" and "Wall of Denial," you've brought in some grooves and feelings that you haven't used in the past.

VAUGHAN I keep trying to make it all come out. I can't read or write music, so sometimes, in trying to find things, I just stick my hand on the neck. Sometimes it's a surprise, and sometimes it becomes what I wanted to hear. I visualize things—sometimes I visualize correctly, and sometimes I don't. As a result, some of my favorite things to play started as mistakes.

GW Are there specific things you'd like to get on record that you haven't yet?

VAUGHAN There are phase capabilities that I'm trying to learn how to use. When something is out of phase, I don't know how to go about making it work *for* me. The engineers usually say, "Oops, this is out of phase; can't use that." There are different qualities to that, and it seems to me that you could make that work, somehow.

Different effects make things go in and out of phase. Y-jacking two amps [*using a y-cable to run one guitar direct to two amps*] can put them in phase with each other, but as soon as you send an effect to only one of the amps, the other amp is then out of phase. Some Fuzz Faces make it go one way on a scope, and some make it go the other way. It's just what's happening with the tone. I may be all wet with that, but that seems like the case. There are different sounds that I'm going for. I'm just now learning how to use the studio.

I've got to go pick up Whipper from the airport, so I'll call you back from the car.

GW [*Ten minutes later*] What kind of car are you in?

VAUGHAN A Cadillac.

GW Sounds like a Cadillac. Has there been any talk of releasing any of the live radio broadcasts that you've done?

VAUGHAN Some of them have been bootlegged, and actually bootlegged off of the broadcast masters. That kind of pissed us off. Supposedly, there were no master tapes other than the two-track, but these bootlegs have been remixed. [*laughs*] It was really from the 24-track master tapes in the truck. We'd seen the 24-track running when we did the soundcheck, but they said, "Oh no, that's something else." It was kind of a drag. When we're not being compensated for it, and we didn't plan on it going out, and the contract says it's not, then it shouldn't be. We're trying to locate the tapes now, which is going to be hell to do. Of course, nobody will let anyone know that they've got 'em. We see 'em pop up every once in a while as bootlegs, with new covers.

GW Are there any specific radio broadcasts you'd like to release?

VAUGHAN There's one we did years and years ago in Austin [*released as* In the Beginning], before we ever had a deal or a manager. For several years, the version of "Tin Pan Alley" was the number-one requested song at the radio station. It was about an eight- or nine-minute version, real slow and real quiet. They played it over and over for years, and it's one of my favorites. We may release it, but we just did the live album [Live Alive], so now would be a funny time to release it.

GW I've heard that you're not happy with the live album.

VAUGHAN Well, God, I wasn't in very good shape. I didn't realize how bad a shape I was in at the time. There were more fix-it jobs done on the album than I would have liked.

GW I think "Texas Flood" is a shining moment.

VAUGHAN That was from the Montreux Jazz Festival, and we felt good about what we were doing. Overall, there were some good nights and some good gigs, but it was more haphazard than we would have liked.

GW Have you done any work on movie soundtracks?

VAUGHAN A year and a half ago, we recorded [*The Beatles'*] "Taxman" for an animated film. The whole story line was based on Beatles songs, with various bands doing various songs. The movie hasn't come out.

GW The version of "Pipeline" that you did with Dick Dale for *Back to the Beach* [*1987, with Frankie Avalon and Annette Funicello*] was great.

VAUGHAN That was fun to do. I never met him until we did the filming; he'd already recorded his part, and then I went in and did my part; we never saw each other in the studio. Soundtracks are fun but, right now, I don't know when we'd have the time to do it. I love to play to the picture tube. I loved doing the music to the baseball sequence in *Gung Ho* [*1986, with Michael Keaton*].

GW What would you put on your "essential listening" list?

VAUGHAN Buddy Guy's *A Man and the Blues*, even though he himself doesn't like the record [*laughs*], B.B. King's *Live at the Regal*, Grant Green's *Live at the Lighthouse*—it's not blues, but it's wonderful—and anything by Donny Hathaway, especially the *Donny Hathaway: Live* album; it *kills* me. There's a lot of gospel stuff that I love, but not necessarily up-to-date stuff. People sometimes turn me on to things that aren't new at all.

Of course, I love a lot of Albert King, but I don't know what my favorite would be. There's all kinds of stuff. Hendrix kind of goes without saying. I like just about everything by him. Keep in mind that I go through phases with all of these people, and phases with what I listen to. It's not that I think one is more important than the other; it has to do with what I can take in. I can't take it all in at once. I haven't been home for a while, and I need to dig back into my records.

GW How did you come to use Gibson bass frets, and what are your exact string gauges?

VAUGHAN I started using the different frets because I wore out regular guitar frets so fast. I noticed that I had an easier time playing when I had a little bit more fret. I found out that I could put on bigger frets, raise the strings up and put bigger strings on. To me, it felt *easier* to play. The guitar feels more responsive, because I can play harder. The strings don't crap out, and I don't tear 'em off, and it just works out for me. The gauges vary; it depends on what kind of shape my fingers are in. I go from .011 to .013 for the high E, and that's usually the only one that I change to something lighter. As a rule, the rest of the strings are .015 for the B, .019 for the G, .028 for the D, .038 for the A and .054, .056 or .058 for the low E. You pop 'em, and they stay there.

Well, listen, it's time for Whipper's plane to get here, so I've got to go.

[9]

"That band–the four of us–represents the height of my musical life."

—*TOMMY SHANNON*

RISE AND SHINE

On the occasion of *Blues at Sunrise*, a collection of slew blues classics and previously unreleased gems from Stevie Ray Vaughan and Double Trouble, Tommy Shannon, Chris Layton and Reese Wynans sit down together about their late friend and close musical compatriot.

BY ANDY ALEDORT

CHRIS "WHIPPER" LAYTON, drummer for the legendary blues-rock ensemble Stevie Ray Vaughan and Double Trouble, is horizontally immersed in a large, soft couch in the lounge of Arlyn Studios in Austin, Texas. His rest is well-deserved: during the past weeks, he and fellow Double Trouble bandmate, bassist Tommy Shannon, have been here hard at work recording their first Double Trouble & Friends album, whose numerous guest artists includes Double Trouble keyboardist Reese Wynans.

But Layton's repose is merely temporary: the album still has to be mixed. For the past few minutes, the sound of one of the album's tracks—"In the Garden," a powerfully soulful track featuring singer/

guitarist Susan Tedeschi—has been emanating from the control room. Finally, his curiosity getting the better of him, Layton lifts his head.

"What are y'all doin' in there?" he calls out.

Wynans ambles in from the control room. "We're just listening back to the two different versions of the piano track on this song's outro," he drawls. "We're trying to figure out how to get from one take to the other. We decided that the first take was cool, so we're going to splice that into the second take and then go back to the first one."

"Oh, yeah," says Layton, nodding as he envisions the sound. "I dug that first one, too. It was...kinda *wild.*"

Tommy Shannon suddenly appears from out of nowhere, his imposing six-foot-three frame filling the doorway to the lounge area. "Hey!" he growls, with a grin on his face. "Don't you guys be making any important decisions without me being informed!"

The camaraderie among the three men is undeniable, the result of many years spent together in clubs, studios and concert halls around the world. Layton and Shannon became members of Stevie Ray Vaughan and Double Trouble in 1980; five years later, they were joined by Reese during the recording of the band's third album, *Soul to Soul.* Over the following five years, the four musicians logged many miles together on the road and released two other multi-Platinum SRV albums, *Live Alive* (1986) and *In Step* (1989).

But since Vaughan's death in a helicopter crash in 1990, Layton and Shannon have worked with Wynans only on occasion. Considering that the Double Trouble & Friends album features a virtual who's-who of the greatest blues and R&B players and singers today—including Eric Johnson, Kenny Wayne Shepherd and the Grammy-nominated Tedeschi—there could be no better excuse for the three men to reunite.

"I love Reese—he's just incredible," Shannon says with enthusiasm. "Reese's playing always killed me, and he sounds better than ever. We knew that if we were going to make a Double Trouble & Friends album, he would *have* to be on it."

Always ready to seize an opportunity, *Guitar World* used this rare reunion to conduct an unprecedented three-way interview with Chris, Tommy and Reese to discuss *Blues at Sunrise*, Epic's latest Stevie Ray Vaughan and Double Trouble compilation. The album focuses on the group's greatest recordings of burning slow blues, including *Soul to Soul*'s "Ain't Gone 'N' Give Up on Love," *In Step*'s "Leave My Girl Alone," *The Sky Is Crying*'s "May I Have a Talk with You" and *Texas Flood*'s "Dirty Pool."

Also featured in this career-spanning retrospective is a handful of previously unreleased masterpieces, such as a smoking live version of "Tin Pan Alley," recorded in Montreux, Switzerland, on July 15, 1985 (featuring the late, great blues master Johnny Copeland), and a white-hot alternate take of "The Sky Is Crying." The collection ends with the album's title track, culled from a historic live recording of Stevie Ray with his hero, Albert King, originally broadcast on Canadian television on December 6, 1983 (available in its entirety on *In Session: Albert King with Stevie Ray Vaughan*).

While the idea of compiling an entire album of slow blues might seem somewhat indulgent, *Blues at Sunrise* is remarkably exciting and explosive. In fact, one could argue the depth and scope of Stevie Ray Vaughan's masterful virtuosity is at its most striking within the wide-open context of the slow burners found on this album. One of the best examples is the live version of "Texas Flood," originally found on the *Live at El Mocambo* video. Here, Stevie moves skillfully from the razor-sharp intensity of

Albert King–style phrases to the more delicate, jazzy sounds of T-Bone Walker, only to turn on a dime and crank the fervor up to the realms of Jimi Hendrix.

Squeezing a few breaks from the feverish schedule to complete the Double Trouble & Friends record, Chris, Tommy and Reese took some time out to discuss *Blues at Sunrise* and the powerful guitar mastery of Stevie Ray Vaughan, and to reveal the inner workings of this much-loved and respected band.

GUITAR WORLD *Blues at Sunrise* is a collection of some of the best slow blues performances that Stevie Ray Vaughan and Double Trouble recorded. With that said, a whole record of slow blues doesn't seem like a very exciting idea.

CHRIS LAYTON Those were my thoughts too! [*laughs*] But, actually, when you listen to it as an album, you see that it works really well. The tunes all come from different stages of our career with Stevie, and the songs really stand apart from each other. Each one has its own particular vibe.

GW Can you describe the overall approach that the band took to playing slow blues?

LAYTON A long, long time ago, Stevie and I would talk about blues in general, and sometimes we would talk real specific things. For example, we would talk about Freddie Below, the drummer for Muddy Waters. There are things about Freddie Below's playing that I try to do, like playing a roll into a downbeat, and pulling the time way, way back, so that you come in on the downbeat as late as possible. Then, when you drop in on the downbeat, you really push down on it. It sounds like you are sucking in all of your breath, holding it, and then—"Ahhhhhhh..."—releasing it. We'd talk about those things as concepts. It sounds intellectual to call those things "concepts," but it's really all about how to *feel* something.

TOMMY SHANNON Just like a lot of bands, we'd sit down and listen to all of the old blues records, pick out certain parts and talk about what was cool about them. When it came time for us to get up and play, those things had just become a part of us; we didn't consciously think about them while we played, and we didn't map out a plan of how to use those influences in our music. When you get up and start playing, the different influences naturally come out.

LAYTON A lot of times, bands will sit around and listen to recordings of themselves, and cop certain things to do all of the time. We would listen to records by other people and say, "Check *that* out." It might have been Stevie and I focusing on the playing of a specific drummer, or Tommy and I talking about a guitar player, as opposed to me focusing only on drummers, or Stevie focusing only on guitar players. We'd kick around all of these different ideas about things, like playing with dynamics as a band. When it was time to play, all of that stuff would work its way out unconsciously.

SHANNON We never tried to copy anything that we heard on a record. We used our influences to learn to play the way we wanted to.

GW Your version of Howlin' Wolf's "May I Have a Talk with You" features a classic blues bass line that includes a chromatically descending line. Is this the same bass line that appears on the original recording?

SHANNON I really don't know. When we recorded that song, I just played the bass line that I thought best fit the music at that time. You'll find that bass line, or a very similar one, on many different old blues records; I didn't learn it from any one specific tune. Sometimes, you'll play the very first thing off the top of your head, and it works fine. You try to find that place where you remain faithful to the music without copying someone else's playing.

REESE WYNANS The way the arrangements came together with Stevie was remarkable. I remember that, when I first joined the band, the only time we rehearsed was when we were recording in the studio! At the very first gig I did, I thought I was just going to come up and play the four or five songs I had played in the studio, and they would play the rest of the set. But Stevie kept me up there the whole time.

We never rehearsed at all, and the arrangements came together purely from the experience of playing live. The arrangements would then grow and change the more we played together. We became more attuned to what each of us was doing on each song, and the arrangements would change accordingly. The arrangements remained "works in progress" and continued to change here and there as time went on.

GW In interviews, Stevie said that he found that approach to be the most natural way to devise an arrangement, although sometimes it didn't work out as well. He said, "Sometimes we'll play and play and play, but it still sounds like we chopped and chopped and chopped."

WYNANS That's one of the toughest things about the blues: how can you rehearse the blues? You could sit around a rehearsal room and say, "This is the way I want to do it," but, as a form, it's "live" music. You don't put the same thing into it in a rehearsal room as you do in front of an audience. You have no audience to play off of in a rehearsal room.

LAYTON Stevie always thought that if there was something cool that we did the last time we played a song, we shouldn't try to copy it. What we should do is try to get back to the way we were feeling when we played some other cool, spontaneous thing. That way, something else might come out that was just as cool but entirely different. Whenever you try to re-create a moment, it never works.

WYNANS That's a mistake everyone makes: you try to recapture some specific vibe, and it invariably turns into another kind of animal.

SHANNON With our band, I don't think there were any big plans along the lines of, "Okay, this is the sound we want to have, and this is the kind of band we want to become." The music itself became the guide: we listened, and we followed where it was taking us.

GW Were there any particular challenges to playing different slow blues songs?

WYNANS Slow blues songs are the toughest of all. Stevie loved to stretch out the slow blues tunes when we played live, and we, as a rhythm section, would be thinking, Well, how can we make this slow blues sound different than another slow blues in the set, one that really sounds a lot like it?

SHANNON Oh, I know, I know! [*laughs*]

WYNANS Some guys never figure out how to do that. We would try different things, and we'd end up with an entirely different song. Every one of the slow blues we played was treated its own way. And each one was a jewel.

LAYTON You know what? A while back—I think it was in '92 or '93—CBS International called me because they came across this bootleg of us playing live with Stevie. They wanted someone from the band to help them stop this thing from being released. They asked me to listen to it to see if I could figure out what show it was from. Of course, there were no indicators like, "Hello, Sydney, on January 23rd!" [*laughter*] It was ridiculous to try to figure out the date just from the playing. There were all of these heavy stipulations that I couldn't let anyone hear it, it couldn't be copied and I couldn't discuss it with anyone. Of course, me being me, I didn't copy it. It was really fucking good! There was a "Tin Pan Alley" on there, and a "Texas Flood," and it had some of the best slow blues I've ever heard this band do. And I still kick myself in the ass for not having copied it!

"Stevie always played like he was **pouring his life out.**"

—*TOMMY SHANNON*

SHANNON & WYNANS [*laugh*]

LAYTON It never came out officially, and I never heard anything more about it. Man, it was a good one!

WYNANS The thing is, I don't know how many shows we played as a band. I was in the band for five years, and we did about 100 shows a year. There may have been only one or two weak shows.

LAYTON Paris, 1986? [*laughs*]

WYNANS To my mind, all of the rest of them were all four stars. Was it Paris, or was it Vienna?

SHANNON No, the Olympia Theater is in Paris.

WYNANS Well, that may be the one bad show I can think of. And there was one in Louisiana a couple of weeks before the Paris show. We just weren't on our game.

SHANNON Yeah, but as a general rule in that band—and it was an unspoken rule—when we got there to play, everyone was expected to give it everything they had, with no excuses.

WYNANS No matter what kind of shape you may have been in, you reached deep down into yourself and pulled it out, and got to that spot where you know who you are and just what you are doing. That's where the "show" comes from.

GW Stevie must have been a great example in that department. Chris has always said that, no matter how sick, tired, or worn-out Stevie may have been, he was always able to rally his energies.

SHANNON Yeah, he'd find that one spot inside himself to draw the energy from, and he did it every time. Stevie always played like he was pouring his life out.

WYNANS Once we hit the stage, it was time to turn it out. I can remember getting onstage with a fever and feeling horrible, and I know all of us had moments like that.

SHANNON You couldn't call in sick.

"You go through all kinds of trials in your life, but **the love of playing never changes.**"
—*TOMMY SHANNON*

LAYTON In other words, we could get up there and kick some ass! [*laughter*] No matter how we felt, we were good. We tried as hard as we could.

GW What would you say are the qualities that make up a great blues performance?

WYNANS It takes different things every time. It usually comes down to someone who plays the blues right, and plays it with a feeling. Some guys are "there" all of the time, and some guys are only "there" sometimes. Some of them want to show it all in a single song. After a couple minutes of that, you don't want to hear any more. It's like, stop showing me the same thing over and over!

With the blues, you have to make the audience want more of it. There is always something held back, which makes you want to keep going. And while you're playing, the vibe among the musicians onstage is so important. You're all looking at each other and getting ready to take the music someplace else. Something is going on—the musicians are not just going through the motions.

GW The audience can see that, they can hear that and they can feel that. They are totally aware of when the music is truly spontaneous and "in the moment." With a master like B.B. King, it's all about how the story of the music unfolds, and that's what the people are reacting to.

SHANNON Oh, yeah, that's it. B.B. is a true master. He's never grown tired of it, that's the beauty of it. He loves the music so much. It's like, no matter how old you get, that's the part of you that never changes. You go through all kinds of trials in your life, your ups and downs and all kinds of shit, but the love of playing never changes.

Back when we were with Stevie, in 1988 or 1989, we did this show out in California with Santana and B.B. King. It was total chaos: it was a big stage show, with an elaborate light show and everything, and everyone wanted everything to come off big and powerful, including us. Everyone was going crazy getting things together. So we played, and Santana played, and everything went real well. Then B.B. closed the show.

B.B. came out and started playing, and it was like a slap in the face! It was like someone grabbed you and said, "Wake up!!" Stevie was standing on the side of the stage, watching B.B., and he turned to me and said, "B.B. is giving me a spanking tonight!" He told B.B. that, too. We were watching them, and they were playing like they were in no hurry, like, "I ain't goin' nowhere—I'm right here. Everything's cool—nothing to get excited about." They were just playing their asses off. Listening to the simplicity and beauty of B.B.'s playing is a real experience.

GW Did Double Trouble's approach to playing the blues evolve over time?

LAYTON We never really talked about how we should play anything. Other than commenting about any one player's style, the one thing that we did talk about was groove. If Stevie would play a record for me and say, "Hey, check this out," I knew that that's how he liked to hear it, and how he thought of the sound of certain things. He would never say, "Play like the way this guy plays." We listened to so much different stuff, and that helped us figure out our own approach and how to interpret other players' styles.

GW Chris, when you first got together with Stevie, wasn't it with a larger band?

LAYTON That's right. We had a sax player, Johnny Reno, and a "featured" singer, Lou Ann Barton. At that point, we were playing stuff that sounded like R&B-type blues, like Slim Harpo's "Ti Na Ni Na Nu" and things like that. That band was never recorded properly, but I've got bootlegs. It's not that Stevie was playing more reserved then, it's that he was playing more blues/R&B/part-oriented stuff.

GW And the volume of the music was much lower.

LAYTON Lou Ann wasn't into it when it got loud and into Jimi Hendrix territory. By the time she left the band, Johnny Reno had already left, so it was down to Stevie, me, and bassist Jack Newhouse. Then Jack left and we got Tommy. At that point, we played full-on, rocked-out blues, plus Jimi Hendrix and whatever we wanted to do.

SHANNON That's exactly what it was: a wide-open field.

LAYTON No limits...no holds barred.

GW Something really great about a trio is that, compared to a four-piece, there is so much more room to fill, and it can be filled in so many different ways.

SHANNON That's right. And we didn't just listen to straight blues. That wasn't the only thing that influenced us, even in terms of playing the blues. The influences of other styles of music would have an effect on how we played the blues, too. For instance, the Donny Hathaway *Live* album was, collectively, one of the band's favorite records. We also went through a period where all we listened to on the tour bus was George Jones.

LAYTON We would also listen to Stevie Wonder all of the time.

SHANNON All of those different sounds and styles had an influence on our playing. And we listened to a lot of Hendrix, of course.

GW Can you describe how the vibe of the music on the Donny Hathaway *Live* album affected the music you were playing?

LAYTON There is a song on that album, "What's Going On," that I have played so many times, just sitting and jamming along with the stereo. The groove [*drummer*] Freddie White plays on that song has gotten into just about every groove that I play!

SHANNON I've practiced along to that record since it first came out, off and on. That record features the ultimate rhythm section, if you ask me. The bass player, Willie Weeks, is a friend of mine, and he's probably my favorite bassist.

GW So, you guys are talking about the feel of the music as an element of musical language to be influenced by and to bring into your own music?

SHANNON Yes. I look at music as this big melting pot: you listen to all of these different things that you really like, and you listen to all of these parts over and over again, and they overwhelm you. It gives you such a great feeling. You back the tape up and listen to those parts over and over, focusing on all the little subtleties. It all goes into this melting pot, and when you start playing, little bits and pieces of it come out in different ways. And it's your own way. That's in line with the evolution of our band with Stevie.

LAYTON There's a song that's going to be on our Double Trouble & Friends album, called "Turn Toward the Mirror," which features the Arc Angels lineup of Charlie Sexton, Doyle Bramhall, Jr., Tommy and me. It's a rock song, but during the verse section I'm playing the "What's Going On" beat as a "rock" idea, as opposed to a funk/R&B idea.

GW You are talking about very subtle elements in the rhythms, right?

LAYTON Right. It's rock, but it still has the "swing" of funky R&B.

SHANNON And you don't even think about it. You've heard these sounds so much, they just become a part of you. Another song on our upcoming record, "In the Garden," is based on a rhythmic syncopation that I first learned from Willie Weeks. You can hear those rhythms in my playing a lot.

GW All of those elements can be traced back to the source. Rock and roll rhythm sections had a certain feel in the Fifties, and that changed in the Sixties with R&B and soul. And the rock music of the late Sixties and early Seventies expanded the qualities of the groove even further. How those rhythmic elements are used within a new context helps to create new music.

SHANNON Absolutely. We felt free to bring in whatever influences we pleased.

LAYTON When Tommy joined the band, the only thing that guided our music was whether we were moved by it. If we weren't moved by it, then we weren't moving in the right direction. Before that happened, we were more uncertain, and we'd discuss our music almost in terms of radio formats, like "this should be more R&B" or "this should be more blues." Even playing straight blues, what gave our trio an original sound was that we didn't have any of those guidelines. We never said, "Well, we're more of a blues band" or "We have to do more of this or that." When it felt good and it really clicked, we knew that was our thing.

GW Did success give you the freedom to explore whatever avenues you wanted, and just play?

LAYTON I don't know if that's really the best way to describe it. Being more successful meant that you put more records out, and people bought them and they wanted to hear you do those songs the way you had done them on the records. You feel some obligation there. Before that, we would play anything and everything that came to mind.

SHANNON Speaking for myself, it was reassuring when we began to achieve success; our hard efforts had been justified in that way. We knew that people liked what we were doing, and it made our job that much easier. Things happened to the music just from time having gone by and from our having played together for so long. Over time, we shed the skin of trying to be a "blues band," and we became something else from playing what we loved and trusting our instincts, which helped us to grow in a different way.

GW Even as a trio, the band sounded a lot different in '82 compared to the way it sounded in '85.

SHANNON Yeah. We got a lot heavier!

LAYTON There were times in the real early days, like back in '79, that just Stevie and I would play gigs together—just drums and guitar. There's this little place called Magnolia that used to be called the Austex Lounge, and me and Stevie would go in there on a Wednesday night and play for free to about five people! It was a real fuckin' dump—there weren't even any windows!

SHANNON It was just an old wooden shack.

LAYTON The door had a little diamond-shaped window in it; that was the only way you could see what was going on in the outside world—

or see in! We'd do "Chitlins Con Carne," Les McCann/Eddie Harris tunes and "Stang's Swang." We'd play whatever, and people would yell back at us. It was fun!

GW The first cut on *Blues at Sunrise* is "Ain't' Gone 'N' Give Up on Love." The song was originally recorded for *Soul to Soul*, which represents the point at which Reese joined the band.

WYNANS That's right. "Ain't Gone 'N' Give Up on Love" was one of Stevie's originals, and it was one he really liked. We played it at almost every show. It's not just a traditional 12-bar blues because it has a really cool bridge in it, and the solo comes in on the IV chord. For the bridge, we wrote this arrangement that built up, and we put all of these cool little things in there. We have the chord inversions on the bridge, with the thirds in the bass, and that supplies the big build-up into the solo. Those things made the song really special. And the lyric was a positive kind of message that meant a lot to Stevie.

LAYTON [*quoting*] "Little Johnny Taylor told us oh so long ago...done all of the midnight crying, all the cheatin' and lyin'..."

SHANNON It was originally, "I'm Going to Give Up on Love," wasn't it?

LAYTON No, uh-uh. "Ain't Gone 'N' Give Up on Love" means "I'm not going to give up on love."

SHANNON Well, I know that! You don't have to spell it out for me! [*laughter*] I think I get it!

LAYTON One of my favorite things about that tune is that Stevie added six-string bass to the verse sections for this little strummed chord on the first beat of each bar. He had put a paper matchbook cover over the bridge saddles to give it that muted sound. We used to call him "Modern Man" for coming up with crazy things like that.

GW When Reese joined the band, I think the sound of the band changed again, because now there was room for Stevie not to play at all. He could just stand there and sing, like B.B. or Albert King, and play the guitar licks in between the vocal phrases. Reese's presence had a major effect on the sound of the music.

WYNANS A lot of keyboard players want to completely remold everything when they join a band, but I thought it was a great band to begin with, and I just wanted to "play along" with what they were doing. Stevie didn't want to have to play rhythm all of the time when he was singing because he wanted to be able to concentrate more on the singing. When I joined, he was able to do that, and Chris, Tommy and I could focus more on the groove, and form a tight three-piece rhythm section.

GW The remnants of the "trio" concept are still intact on *Soul to Soul*, with the evidence of some real heavy rhythm guitar. By the time of *In Step*, the music had really changed a lot as a keyboard-bass-drum rhythm section fronted by the singer/guitarist became the structure of the band's sound. And the sound of the band live changed a lot, too; Stevie definitely left more space, which resulted in a "clearer" sonic picture.

> "Each song was its **own personal statement.**"
> —*REESE WYNANS*

WYNANS That's very true. I felt that my job was to make the change from a three-piece to a four-piece as subtle as possible. And then the sound of the band evolved in a natural way over time.

SHANNON When Reese joined, it took a load off of me. I could play a little less and concentrate more on the groove and play in a slightly different style.

WYNANS The most interesting thing to me about the songs on *Blues at Sunrise* is that they are all basically 12-bar blues, but each one is played with a very different approach and sound. "Ain't Gone 'N' Give Up on Love" is completely different from "Texas Flood," for example. We did "Texas Flood" like an anthem! It was a slow blues, but when we played it, it was a monster slow blues. It was a huge thing. "Ain't Gone 'N' Give Up on Love" is more of a cool-groove, T-Bone Walker kind of a blues. "Tin Pan Alley" was a real mean, sparse minor blues. "The Things (That) I Used to Do," originally by Guitar Slim, had more of a 6/8 kind of feel to it, as opposed to the 12/8 feel of most slow blues. That gives the song a completely different feel.

I remember Tommy and I talking about how we didn't want to play the same parts as we had done on other slow blues, and we consciously did what we could to give each song its own distinctive treatment. That's exactly what made each of these slow blues songs work. I don't know that a lot of bands would take the time and the effort to do that.

SHANNON That was the challenge of it, and we loved the challenge. The goal was to make them each sound different, without losing the feel. Each one had to be different, because we often played many of these songs within the context of a single set.

WYNANS Of course, Stevie's part was different every night, because he had all of the licks and all of the singing to do. We wanted him to be able to do his thing while we supplied a different backdrop each time. Each song was its own personal statement. And I think it worked out pretty good.

GW This isn't the first time you guys have worked together since playing with Stevie. You also did the two Kenny Wayne Shepherd albums together [*Trouble Is...* and *Live On*], and a record with Buddy

Guy's guitar player, Scott Holt. How would you describe the vibe that happens when the three of you get together to play?

WYNANS Back in the Eighties, we practically lived together all of the time. We played together all over the world, and we really got to know each other as musicians and as people. Even after not seeing these guys for years and only working together occasionally, I feel the energy and enthusiasm that we built from the old days immediately. I walk in now, all these years later, and I'm right there; I can still feel that same great vibe that we had 10, 15 years ago. I thought our band was a great band, and it still is a great band. I love playing with these guys. We worked so much together that we've established our bond, and it's just there.

SHANNON Yep, that's very true. That band— Stevie Ray Vaughan and Double Trouble, with the four of us—represents the height of my musical life. The chemistry of it was like "one plus one equals five." It wouldn't have worked like it did had we not really cared about each other. We were like brothers.

"I've heard Stevie play with other musicians that I think are better than myself, **but it didn't sound the same.**"
—*TOMMY SHANNON*

WYNANS The energy and the good vibes were obvious.

LAYTON Many people don't understand that that's what made that band work. We were like a family, really. I've been in other bands that were more like going to a job site. Some people view their musical relationships like they do their other relationships, and that's a little different for everyone. We all viewed this band as a family, as opposed to a business arrangement. The music became something else that we happened to do together, because we liked being with each other anyway. I mean, the music was the primary reason we were together, obviously, but it wasn't like we would have no reason to hang out together if we weren't playing.

SHANNON It was all about the underlying attitude, the feeling that drove all of that, which was the love for the music, the love for each other and the common goal that we shared. We were all reaching for the same level of musical fulfillment.

WYNANS I should also say that I think Stevie realized that he could have played with anyone. I'm obviously not the best keyboard player in the world; there's a lot of guys that could sweep me right under the table, and he could have worked with any of them. But we all cared a lot about the music, and there was a special feeling there. You never know if that's going to be there with other players.

GW As an outsider looking in, I think that tight spiritual bond between all of you was obvious and had a major effect on the way the music spoke to the audience.

WYNANS That will happen with a band every once in a while. Neil Young and Crazy Horse is a good example of a band that created something very special, something that would only happen with those specific guys. There are not many bands like that.

GW And you couldn't replace even one of you, because the dynamic would be completely different.

SHANNON That's right. I've heard Stevie play with other musicians that I think are better than myself, but it didn't sound the same. The connection wasn't there.

WYNANS And the connection is the weird part. That's the thing that can't be explained. Because it's just there.

SHANNON Anytime someone would sit in with our band—which didn't happen a lot—after a couple of songs, Stevie would be uneasy. He'd look over at one of us, and we knew what he was thinking. He wanted to get back to the core.

LAYTON We played together for so long just of the love of it—because, in the beginning, and for quite a while, we sure as hell weren't making any money from it. We were so broke. Success to me meant that I'd be able to buy a car, or not worry about whether I should pay the gas bill instead of the electric bill 'cause I could only afford to pay one of them. I didn't want to live like that. Then there are all of the self-doubts: "Does this music mean anything to anyone other than me? I'd like to think that it would."

You don't get up in the morning and drink a cup of coffee because someone is paying you to do it. You do it without thinking about it. Does someone have to pay you to go eat a meal when you are hungry? No, you go do it because you are hungry for it. That's how playing music always was for us. So, success, for us, really meant that we could live on playing music, and that other people wanted to hear it, too. Everything else is like gravy.

[10]

"That gig catapulted us to
heights we hadn't
yet imagined."
—TOMMY SHANNON

SWISS
MISADVENTURE

The first time Stevie Ray Vaughan played the
Montreux Jazz Festival, he was brutally savaged.
The second time, he was celebrated. Here, his
bandmates recall the tumultuous events surrounding
both performances.

BY ANDY ALEDORT

IT BEGAN AS AN auspicious 45-minute set at Europe's preeminent international music festival. It ended with offers that brought fame and fortune to a trio of young, unknown blues players.

In between, there were enough boos and catcalls to make even the toughest band of musicians crawl off the stage.

The place was the 1982 Montreux Jazz Festival, and the group was no less than Stevie Ray Vaughan and Double Trouble, then an unknown, unsigned three-piece from Austin, Texas. The gig, a spot on the festival's "Blues Night," had been set up by heavyweight record producer Jerry Wexler, who had become a devoted SRV fan after he saw the group perform in Austin earlier that year. For

Vaughan and his bandmates—bassist Tommy Shannon and drummer Chris Layton—the chance to play before an international audience was nothing less than a godsend.

"Getting invited to play at Montreux was like a dream come true for us," says Layton. "Montreux was a big deal; we'd never played a gig anywhere near that prestigious before."

Stevie was characteristically cautious in his appraisal of the opportunity. "Things are starting to happen," he said at the time. "I can't say what'll come out of it, and I wouldn't even try. We'll just have to wait and see."

But even Stevie wasn't prepared for what awaited him and his group at Montreux. Upon taking the stage, the band tore through its opening number, the Freddie King classic "Hideaway," only to be showered at the song's climax with a chorus of boos. A spasm of shock shot through the trio. Could this be happening? Gathering their wits, the band continued through the set of time-honored blues classics, playing with the visceral authority and swagger for which SRV and Double Trouble would soon be known. Still, the catcalls persisted. Eventually, the band left the stage in a state of disbelief.

Two members of the audience were in a state of disbelief as well, but for reasons different from those of Vaughan and his band. Their names: David Bowie and Jackson Browne. Bowie, a Montreux resident, had come to the show specifically to see Stevie at the invitation of Montreux organizer Claude Nobs. To put it mildly, he liked what he saw.

"SRV completely floored me," says Bowie, recalling the show. "I probably hadn't been so gung-ho about a guitar player since seeing Jeff Beck in the early Sixties with his band the Tridents. Stevie was so complete, so vital and inventive with the form." That night, Bowie asked Stevie to play on his next record, the smash hit *Let's Dance,* and join him for a tour. Though Stevie's tour participation in Bowie's tour was derailed, his contributions to *Let's Dance,* particularly on "China Girl," are masterful and invigorating, nearly 20 years on. Says Bowie, "I value the short time we had spent working together as one of the greatest musical experiences of my life."

Jackson Browne also spoke with Stevie after the show. Impressed, and eager to lend a hand, he offered the group free recording time at his L.A.-based Downtown Studios. (A year later, Browne's generous offer would result in *Texas Flood,* SRV and Double Trouble's stunning 1983 debut.)

Having at first been shaken by the reaction of his audience, Stevie Ray was now shaking for an entirely different reason: suddenly, all of the pieces were now in place for him and Double Trouble to explode as a worldwide phenomenon—which is exactly what happened. Fate had turned on a dime, and the springboard was Montreux. As Tommy Shannon notes today, "Sometimes what appear as failures are really successes in disguise."

> "Sometimes what appear as failures are really successes in disguise."
> —*TOMMY SHANNON*

In 1985, just three short years later, Stevie Ray and Double Trouble returned to Montreux as headliners and as one of the biggest bands in rock. Although his star was still on the rise, Stevie had firmly established himself as the most significant and influential blues/rock guitarist of his generation, drawing well-earned comparisons to Jimi Hendrix.

Thankfully, both of SRV and Double Trouble's Montreux performances were beautifully recorded—and filmed. These long-sought-after recordings were finally released as *Stevie Ray Vaughan and Double Trouble—Live in Montreux 1982 and 1985.* In this *Guitar World* exclusive, Chris Layton and Tommy Shannon offer the details of these two incendiary SRV concert events.

GUITAR WORLD How would you describe your first Montreux experience?

CHRIS LAYTON At the time, the very idea of us going to Montreux was so far removed from the scope of where we were at. We were an unsigned band knocking around Texas, having a hard time just trying to make a living. We'd play a gig in Austin one weekend, play Lubbock the next weekend, come back and play Austin, then maybe go over to Houston. Occasionally, we'd go all the way to Dallas. That was about it; we were just bouncing around the clubs.

GW How did you get invited to play Montreux?

LAYTON Lou Ann Barton, who had been the featured singer in an earlier version of Double Trouble, had a record release party at the Continental Club in Austin for her record, *Old Enough.* We were invited to play at the party, and Jerry Wexler was there. Jerry really liked us, and he said to Chesley [*Millikin, Double Trouble's manager*], "Claude Nobs, the organizer of the Montreux Jazz Festival, is a good friend of mine; I think these guys ought to go over there and play. I'll give him a call." Chesley's impression was that Montreux was the center of the music world in Europe. It was a very important festival, and he really wanted us to do it.

GW Did you guys get paid for the gig?

TOMMY SHANNON Yeah, but it wasn't any great deal of money. It didn't come close to covering our expenses. There was no way that the fee for the show would even put a dent in offsetting our costs.

GW Did you wonder if it was worth the trouble of going all the way to Switzerland for one 45-minute set?

LAYTON Chesley said to us, "I have the feeling that this will be the greatest thing for your career. I can feel it in my *bones!*" I said, "What the fuck are you basing that on?" I mean, how could he have any idea? Anyway, we put the numbers together to see what it would cost to get us and a modest amount of gear over there. To my recollection, it was thousands of dollars, like $16,000 in flights, hotels, transportation and shipping. So we booked another gig following Montreux in Basil, Switzerland, just to make the trip a little more worthwhile. We'd been making a few hundred bucks per gig, and the idea of having to go thousands and thousands of dollars into debt was a little daunting. But at the same time, we figured, Okay, let's go way into debt—we can hardly keep our gas and electricity on anyway!

SHANNON We definitely had some well-founded uncertainty about making the trip; there was no reason to think that one gig was going to change our whole lives. But we knew it was too good an opportunity to turn down, no matter what. One of the biggest factors was that Stevie was very excited about going to the Montreux Jazz Festival to play. We were all excited about it, really. At that point in our career as a band, that was the biggest, most important gig we'd ever done.

We got over there and, before our set, Larry Graham [*bassist for Sly & the Family Stone*] asked if he could jam with us on "Johnny B. Goode" for the encore. But there was one problem: we didn't get an encore.

While we played, there were a few people out there booing, but to us it sounded like thousands! We got a mediocre response, at best, and we felt like we were bombing, like we weren't wanted. But Stevie wouldn't let it get to him. He just played his ass off, and he never let up. But when we got offstage, he was broken-hearted. We were all in a state of shock.

GW Didn't Stevie say, "We didn't deserve that. We weren't that bad!"

SHANNON Yes, those were his exact words. We were so wired up to knock 'em out, and we thought we were, until the boos came.

LAYTON The thing that was so fucking out of whack about that gig was the lineup for that night. Just about every other act on the bill was either someone sitting on a stool with an acoustic guitar or steel guitar, accompanied by piano. When we came on, at our normal, fully amplified level, it seemed completely incongruous with what had come before. It was probably the worst setup we ever had. And then, of course, no one knew us from a hole in the wall, either.

> "When we opened for the Clash in our own hometown, **we got spit on!**"
> —*CHRIS LAYTON*

SHANNON We had gone over "Johnny B. Goode" with Larry Graham in the dressing room before we went out. After we were done and went back to the dressing room, he was already rehearsing "Johnny B. Goode" with the next band! [*laughs*]

LAYTON That was like adding insult to injury! It was bad enough getting booed; now Larry Graham won't even play "Johnny B. Goode" with us. And I was thinking, Now we have this massive debt, and we're going back to making $400 a night. [*Moaning*] How are we gonna dig our asses out of this hole?

GW Did you, as a band, feel that the booing was unjust, and that the audience was wrong, plain and simple?

LAYTON Wherever we went, and whatever we did, we were always determined to play with the energy and the force that we knew we could. Being encouraged or discouraged by an audience didn't really prevent that from happening. Whether they loved us or wanted to throw tomatoes, we still played with the same intensity and devotion. When we opened for the Clash in our own hometown, at the Austin Coliseum, we got spit on! Nonetheless, even with circumstances like that, we still put our hearts and souls into our playing no matter what.

SHANNON We believed in what we were doing, and when you do, your dedication cannot be shaken.

GW During the 1985 show, Stevie said to the audience, "The first time we were here, we got booed. First time we were here, we got a Grammy!"

SHANNON That was the ironic part of the whole thing. There we were, feeling like it was the worst gig we'd ever done, and then "Texas Flood" was included on the Atlantic Records compilation *Blues Explosion*. The track ended up winning a Grammy.

LAYTON Sitting here in my house, I am looking at the poster of that first show right now. That gig was an event in our lives that we will never forget, because it was really poignant. We went there and were treated in a way that we never had been before. But that's where we met David Bowie and Jackson Browne, the two guys most responsible for getting the band's career on the right track.

GW Can you characterize Bowie's impact on Stevie's career?

LAYTON Playing on Bowie's *Let's Dance* album was a tremendous career boost for Stevie and for us. He was heard by millions of people, virtually overnight.

SHANNON Jackson Browne gave us the use of his studio, and those recordings became our very first album, *Texas Flood*, which has since earned the stature as a landmark blues album.

LAYTON It proved to be a huge episode in my life, and in all of our lives, because you can wrap all of these things into that one gig. I will never forget that night; it's the most significant gig I've ever done. All of the stuff that happened from that one gig is all of the stuff you pray for. As a dedicated musician, you want to play good music, be successful at it and make records that people like and buy.

GW Irrespective of the crowd reaction, it seems that all of the pieces were in place: you showed up and played, and the people that needed to hear you right then were there, too.

SHANNON From my philosophical point of view, I believe that things don't happen by accident. At that point in our lives, playing that festival was the beginning of the next phase of our careers and all that happened later on. All of the pieces were in the right place, and that gig catapulted us to heights we hadn't yet imagined.

GW The set you played that night was, "Hideaway/Rude Mood," "Pride and Joy," "Texas Flood," "Love Struck Baby," "Dirty Pool," "Give Me Back My Wig" and "Collins Shuffle." Was that your standard set at the time?

LAYTON Pretty much, but we did more songs than that per set in a regular bar gig. We felt those songs represented the cream of the crop—the best of what our music was about.

GW How did that "Hideaway/Rude Mood" arrangement develop?

SHANNON It was purely spontaneous, which is how everything was when we played with Stevie. We didn't discuss arrangement ideas; if we played something once and liked it, it became part of the standard arrangement, until it morphed into something else. Things like that just grew from us playing together and letting the music go wherever it would.

LAYTON The "Hideaway/Rude Mood" combination went through all kinds of transformations. One time, Stevie stuck his hand out in the middle of "Hideaway" signaling us to stop, and he went right into "Rude Mood." We all dug it, so that became the arrangement. That was our M.O. as a band, and it is something I really miss. With Stevie, anything that happened in the songs was the result of how he was feeling it onstage, right there in the moment. Every bit of it was spontaneous, which was cool. You had to get into a certain mental space to pull it off, and that's a great place for a band to be. It's all about being in the moment.

GW Stevie's mastery of Albert King's style is showcased in both the 1982 and 1985 shows, with "Texas Flood" and "Ain't Gone 'N' Give Up on Love," respectively. No one has ever zoned in on Albert's playing like Stevie had. Did Stevie ever discuss his love for and dedication to Albert's style?

LAYTON Stevie always liked to say that he was Albert's white godson.

SHANNON Stevie used to tell the story about the first time he sat in with Albert, at Antone's in Austin, when Stevie was still a teenager. While Stevie was soloing, Albert had a nail file out, filing his nails, like he couldn't have cared less! [*laughs*] But that was a routine of his. He loved Stevie, and he remembered that night years later, when they met again after Stevie had made it.

Cutter Brandenburg, one of Stevie's best friends, used to say, "I don't get it: Stevie says not only does he want to be a black guy, he wants to be an *old* black guy!"

GW When you went back to Montreux in 1985, did any of you harbor any weird feelings, because of the initial negative crowd reaction?

LAYTON By 1985, everything had really changed for us. We went back as the headliner. I did think about our first time there, but the truth is that all of those great things had happened for us because of that first visit.

SHANNON When we went back, our reception was great. There was the prestige of playing Montreux as headliners, so we were very psyched about it.

LAYTON That gig was actually the very last show of a two-week tour in which we'd been to 11 different countries. We had been working hard by that gig, and it was nice to get a little time off right after it.

GW Reese Wynans, your keyboard player, had very recently joined the band at that point, right?

LAYTON Yes. He came in during the recording of *Soul to Soul*, about two or three months before that. So he was a new addition.

GW How would you describe the vibe of the band at that time?

SHANNON We were really riding high. Our career was going great, we were selling a lot of records, and we all felt great about where we were at. It was a good time for us, musically, as a band.

LAYTON Quite honestly, when we went back, I thought about what had happened the first time. By 1985, everything had changed so much. The band was sounding great, we were going back as headliners, and things were going so well for us in every way. In a way, though, it was almost like "just another gig," because we were working so much.

SHANNON That's true.

LAYTON People ask us, "Do you remember when you played that show at such and such?" and the truth is, it's almost impossible to remember anything specific about one gig during a 60-gig tour. But playing Montreux stood out, of course, because, no matter what, it was a special gig.

GW You played songs like "Texas Flood" and "Pride and Joy" at both shows. Had your approach to playing these songs, and this music overall, changed by 1985?

SHANNON Yeah, I think it had. By '85, we evolved into something closer to what we eventually became in 1989, around the time of *In Step*. If you listen to us in '82, we were pretty much a straight blues band, with an edge. Gradually, along the way, Stevie started adding some Hendrix stuff, and we became more powerful. We were still playing blues, but we crossed over a line and brought to it a completely different attitude. Early on, Stevie was afraid to cross that line, because he was concerned about what the blues purists would think. When he finally crossed on over, it was really a cool thing, because what we were doing was like a "new" music. It was blues, but it had the power of a big rock band.

GW The switch from a trio to a four-piece radically changed the sound of the band, and the arrangement concepts, too.

SHANNON As a bass player, the addition of keyboards left me more room; I didn't have to play as much if I didn't want to. In a trio, you have to keep the music sounding full all of the time. But playing in a trio is probably my favorite thing to do. With Reese, we'd gone through a change in our music, and it was cool to interact with four people instead of three.

LAYTON Playing in a trio is like working in primary colors, and with a quartet, you can get into all kinds of different shades. But there is something really magical about a trio.

GW The 1985 show also features the late blues guitar great Johnny Copeland, who sits in on "Tin Pan Alley," a track also included on Stevie's *Blues at Sunrise* album.

SHANNON Stevie dug Johnny Copeland. They used to play together in Houston a lot. Stevie plays on Johnny's *Texas Twister* album, on the song "Don't Stop by the Creek, Son," which is a song we played that night.

LAYTON Johnny was a great guy, really fun to play with. He was in Montreux to do his own show, so we were happy to have him sit in. It was always like that: whoever was around, we'd ask, "Where's your guitar?"

GW This set includes "Gone Home," making it the first-ever release of a live version of this tune.

LAYTON "Gone Home" was definitely an unusual tune for us to play live. We had just cut it for *Soul to Soul*, so we played it live for a little while.

SHANNON That's a song that didn't seem to translate live as well as we would have liked, so we soon dropped it. As time went on, we'd find ourselves gravitating toward certain groups of songs, so, for the most part, that set is representative of our normal set at the time.

GW Do you think this new release offers fans a clearer picture of what Stevie Ray Vaughan and Double Trouble was all about?

SHANNON I do, in a way. Each of those shows represents important steps in our journey as a band. In 1982, no one knew who we were; we were a brand-new band. When we came back in 1985, we were well on our way to the top and feeling great. It's definitely cool to have both aspects of the band—and both aspects of Stevie—right there, side by side.

[11]

"Stevie's level of precision and expertise **was flawless.**"
—*RICHARD MULLEN*

FLOOD ON THE TRACKS

Producer/engineer Richard Mullen details how he
captured Stevie Ray's incredible guitar sound.

"IF YOU GOT CLOSE ENOUGH to Stevie while he was really doing his thing, it was almost like he was in a trance, like something else was playing *through* him. On the spot, Stevie could play things that he'd never done before, like he was tapped into a higher plane. His level of precision and expertise was flawless."

Producer/engineer Richard Mullen is well qualified to speak about the incendiary power and glory of Stevie Ray Vaughan—he was, after all, the man behind the boards for *Texas Flood, Couldn't Stand the Weather, Soul to Soul, In Step, The Sky Is Crying* and *Live at Carnegie Hall*. A guitarist and pedal steel player, Mullen moved to Austin in the early Seventies, and in 1976 connected with a young Stevie Ray

Vaughan, initiating a fruitful relationship that lasted throughout Stevie's career. Mullen's long list of engineering credits include Eric Johnson's landmark 1990 release, *Ah Via Musicom*, and he continues to work with Johnson today.

In conversation, Mullen's respect and admiration for Stevie's artistry is overflowing. "He played on at least a 95 to 98 percent level of perfection all the time," Mullen says of the guitarist. "In the studio, whether he would 'bring it' was not even an issue. He was fearless when it came to playing, and he always played well." Regarding *Texas Flood* and *Couldn't Stand the Weather*, Mullen states, "Every take was based on Stevie's performance. If he exploded on the track, that's the one we used. On every record I made with him, the final product consisted primarily of live takes, which is something above and beyond what most musicians are capable of."

In this extremely rare interview, Richard Mullen describes his approach to recording Stevie Ray, as well as their close working relationship over the course of SRV's life.

GUITAR WORLD How did you make your acquaintance with Stevie?
RICHARD MULLEN I was playing in an original band in Austin called Denim, which I worked with from '73 to '79. The main place we played was the Rome Inn, where we often crossed paths with Stevie, starting in '76 when he was with Paul Ray and the Cobras. This is where Stevie and I had our first conversations. He was very shy, and I think the first three times we spoke we had exactly the same conversation!

I often ran sound at the Rome Inn during those days and would record the shows. I was running sound one night when Paul Ray had gotten sick, and this was literally the very first time Stevie came out as the frontman, doing all the singing. You could see where he was headed. Unfortunately, that tape was stolen!

Stevie was always one of my favorite people to go hear, but his soundmen were so bad. If I were planning to see him, I'd go down to the club in the afternoon and do the soundcheck so that it would sound reasonable when I went to see him that night.

GW You did this for selfish reasons, then?

MULLEN In a way, yes. [*laughs*] I did want it to sound as good as possible, and he noticed that it sounded better when I came down. I eventually moved into live sound and studio work entirely, and a mutual friend of ours, Jan Beaman, who cooked at [*the Austin nightclub*] the Armadillo said, "You and Stevie ought to be working together." So I began doing live sound for him in '81.

GW Was Stevie working with his manager, Chesley Millikin, by this point?

MULLEN Yes. Chesley was responsible for some stuff happening that I wasn't happy about, but he made some good things happen, too. He hooked up the recording session at Jackson Browne's studio, which may have happened partially because he was dating Jackson's sister.

GW You mean we have Jackson's sister to thank for *Texas Flood*?

MULLEN Well, insomuch as she was the connection that got us to Jackson's studio. Chesley did everything in his power to keep me away from that session, but he failed!

GW Was *Texas Flood* the first time you recorded Stevie in the studio?

MULLEN I had used Stevie on some of my own sessions. One was for a singer/songwriter named Vince Bell. I brought Stevie in to do some slide work. The session that turned out to be *Texas Flood* was the first time I worked with Stevie on a session of his own.

GW Did you squeeze into the milk truck for the trip out to L.A.?

MULLEN No, thankfully! Stevie and I had planned to go out there together, but things never work out the way they are supposed to.

Chesley wouldn't have paid my way out there, but I was already in L.A. working in the studio with [*Eighties pop singer-songwriter*] Christopher Cross. I was doing a lot of live touring with him, doing the monitors and the guitar tech work, plus playing and singing, too.

We were finishing up Cross' second record, *Another Page*, and Stevie invited me to the Jackson sessions. In those days, it was common for out-of-town musicians to stay at the Oakland Gardens, so we both were staying at the same place at the same time.

When we met Chesley and Jackson down at the studio, Chesley saw me and pretty much had a heart attack. [*laughs*] I think the main reason he wanted me out of the picture was that he didn't want to ruffle any feathers with Jackson and his engineer. But it turned out that the engineer, Greg Ladanyi, wasn't really interested in the session. Once he'd set things up, he had the assistant run the 24-track machine and that was it. I was just standing in the corner with my hands in my pockets.

They did some recording to get sounds, and Stevie kept looking at me, like, "Help!" He wasn't happy with how it was going, so I said, "Stevie, you are the only one here with any clout. You can change things if you want to." Stevie was always shy back in those days, so a few more hours went by. After going out for some food, we came back and Greg was gone. Stevie went up to the assistant engineer and said, "I brought this guy with me from Texas to do this recording, and we'd really like him to work on it." The assistant said, "I'm just here to punch 'play' and 'record,' so go ahead and do whatever you need to do."

I had a different idea about how to do the session, so I revamped everything, basically starting from scratch: I tuned the drums, set up the guitar and bass, redid the mike placement, re-EQed the board and got new, better sounds for everything. My goal was to make Stevie as happy as possible with his guitar tone, to the point of setting the tones on his amp a certain way. Once I had changed everything around, they were all happy, and all they had to do was go in and play. Whatever they had recorded previously was scrapped.

GW Did you use just one 24-track machine?

MULLEN Yes, but I was really interested in doing it in a 16-track/two-inch format. This way, I could play the tape on my 16-track back home [*at Riverside Sound*] to record the vocals, which is what we ended up doing. Stevie's setup was simple, so we only used 14 tracks, which made it possible for us to use the tape back at my studio.

"I wanted them to play like it was a gig, with **the same sense of abandon.**"

We had recorded a track and were listening back to it when Jackson walked in. He took one look at me and said, "What's going on?" After listening to what we'd done he said, "I don't know exactly what's going on here, but it sounds 100 times better than when I left. You obviously know what you're doing, so the studio is yours for tonight and tomorrow." It was late by then so we broke it down till the next day without having recorded anything to speak of.

GW What other changes had you made to the setup?

MULLEN For one, I put a few go-bos [*partitions*] between the instruments just to prevent the loudness of the guitar amps from killing the drum tracks. But it was pretty much an open space. I wanted the band's "reality" to be as close as possible to what they were used to when they played live. As a matter of fact, I didn't even let them use headphones.

I also wanted them to *play* like it was a gig, with the same sense of abandon. In the recording studio, if you give a musician the chance to think about what they are doing, there's a good chance they'll mess up. I looked at their 14-song set list and said, "Let's go through the tunes just like a set." I wanted it to feel as unstudiolike as possible.

GW Did Stevie sing at all?

MULLEN Only as a cue for the tunes. He knew it wasn't for keeps.

GW How did you mike the instruments?

MULLEN Just one mike on everything. I used two Shure SM-57s on his guitar amps: one on a Fender Vibraverb with a 15-inch Altec Lansing speaker, and one on a Dumble 4x12 bottom with [*Electro-Voice speakers*] connected to a Dumble head. Stevie played through two Vibraverbs, but I only miked one of the speakers in one of them. I positioned the mikes about three or four inches off the cabinet at about a 45-degree angle off the cone.

GW Stevie's sound on *Texas Flood* has been primarily attributed to the Dumble. How did he discover this unusual amplifier?

MULLEN Just prior to the session I stumbled across Jackson's Dumble at a repair shop/rehearsal studio and was blown away by it. This turned out to be Howard Dumble's shop. He and I got together and designed an amp for Christopher Cross called the Steel String Singer, which became an essential part of Stevie's setup for the rest of his career. Eric Johnson used this same amp for many years, too.

GW Did Stevie use the same setup for all of the songs on *Texas Flood*?

MULLEN Yes. The only effect he used was an Ibanez Tube Screamer.

GW Did he use only one guitar for all of the songs?

MULLEN I believe he used only his main guitar, Number One, for the whole record, though he might have used his brown-stain, maple-neck Strat for "Lenny." I wanted them to blow through the tunes as quickly as they could, so we had to keep it simple. The whole record was recorded in two hours—as long as it took to play 14 songs twice. There was no evaluation of the whole thing other than that they were happy with the way it sounded.

GW Was Stevie attuned to the technical aspects of recording?

MULLEN Not at that time, but he did become more attuned later. Stevie could be very finicky about his equipment, but he didn't approach things from a technical point of view—either it felt right or it didn't.

One effect that he liked to use when we mixed *Texas Flood* was this really obscure Roland delay/chorus that gave a little bit of a growl sound. It was a stereo device that created phasing effects, which you can hear on the solo to "Mary Had a Little Lamb" and the end solo on "Pride and Joy." Stevie sat at the board and brought that effect in and out as the song progressed. He used the same effect on *Couldn't Stand the Weather*, too.

GW Were there any specific things he would ask of you as an engineer?

MULLEN Not at the time of *Texas Flood*. He would just play, come in and say, "Sounds good." As time passed and Stevie learned more about recording, he got more particular about things and would say, "Let's try this," something along those lines. To be honest, there were times when this was more of a detriment than a help, like if he suddenly got it in his head to change the snare sound by pulling it apart. When we did *Soul to Soul*, he had me open up a snare and fill it with packing peanuts because he thought it would sound good. It didn't!

GW What happened after you finished recording at Jackson's?

MULLEN We took the tapes to Riverside Sound in Austin, and a few weeks later Stevie came in to record the vocals. I gave him two tracks to work with, and he would cut the vocal part for each song twice. We would use either the best of the two tracks or do a quick comp [*editing parts together from different takes*].

Overall, there was no finagling of anything on *Texas Flood*. It was about as live and true to a performance as it could possibly be. When we were done, I did some mixes and ran off a cassette for Stevie. Those are the mixes that John Hammond heard.

GW At the time, did you feel you'd recorded a great album, or was it more that it was just a good representation of the band?

MULLEN To be honest, we felt we'd done a good job, but it was viewed as a demo that would be used to try to get a deal. Hammond heard it and said, "This is great. Let's just release this."

GW Chris Layton told me that, while Stevie was off rehearsing with David Bowie, he played the tapes for some friends in his hometown of Corpus Christi, and the reaction was, "Well, it's good, but it's just a bunch of shuffles and slow blues. Are people really interested in that kind of music right now?"

MULLEN I think many people in Texas are used to hearing a lot of blues, and they were used to hearing Stevie, who'd been kicking around Texas for a long time. That tape was what Stevie sounded like live. But people from other parts of the country who had never heard him thought, Wow—this guy is really great! It didn't matter that it was a bunch of shuffles; here was a guy that could play with aggression and soul and was a super talent.

GW Do you believe the bare simplicity of *Texas Flood* allowed Stevie's personality to shine through so clearly?

MULLEN That's right. There were no overdubs, and here he was, basically live. That's why I wanted him to approach it like a gig from the beginning, because I knew what he was capable of. I wanted them to feel as comfortable as possible, and I think that comes across when you listen to the record. That was Stevie; you can hear every little nuance in his playing.

GW Did you participate in the final mixes of *Texas Flood*?

MULLEN No. I had some prior commitments, so the final mixes were done by Lincoln Clapp at Media Sound in New York. I thought Stevie might hold that against me, but he didn't. But I do regret not doing it.

GW Following *Texas Flood*, when did you next work with the band?

MULLEN Right before going to New York to record *Couldn't Stand the Weather*, Stevie booked a rehearsal hall in Austin for about three weeks to do preproduction stuff, like writing songs. Then we went up to the Power Station in New York to record.

GW How did these sessions differ from *Texas Flood*?

MULLEN This was really the first time they were going to a studio to make a record, and they weren't as "innocent" as they had been. From a production point of view it was a lot more difficult to make *Couldn't Stand the Weather* simply because they were unsure about what they wanted to do. As soon as the first record was done, they hit the road and they were nonstop until they came in to do the second record. They didn't really have any time to prepare. They had some different ideas, with only pieces of songs written.

There were probably 5,000 different song lists. The joke of the sessions was that every time Stevie went off to do a line [*of cocaine*], he'd come back with a different list. I was guilty of the same thing.

GW Did you utilize more tracks for *Couldn't Stand the Weather* than *Texas Flood*?

MULLEN Not really; we just used one 24-track machine. Most of the songs were just the trio, but the title track and "The Things (That) I Used to Do" both feature Stevie's brother, Jimmie, on rhythm guitar. We might have added a few more room mikes on the drums, but we were still looking at about 20 tracks [*in use*]. In this situation, those extra tracks were for additional takes, but Stevie was so good you just plain didn't need 'em.

One of the only overdubs on *Couldn't Stand the Weather* was on "Stang's Swang." Stevie sat in the control room and redid his guitar part, mostly because he used a big-box jazz guitar, like a Johnny Smith, and he wanted to sit by the board to make tonal adjustments. He also used a different amp on that track, a Roland JC-120, which was unusual for him.

The only other punch [*an overdub made while the tape is rolling*] I can think of is during the "Couldn't Stand the Weather" guitar solo, on the chord change from D to Bm. He may have switched to different guitar right there.

GW For *Couldn't Stand the Weather*, did he use different guitars from what he used on *Texas Flood*?

MULLEN He had more of a collection by then, but at that time he favored Number One over anything else. I was very vocal about him using that guitar, because I think he had the most authority and the best sound on it.

GW He would punch that guitar and it would respond in a way that *was* the Stevie Ray Vaughan sound.

MULLEN There was a depth to the sound of that guitar. He could slam it or pick it gently, and it always had a huge tone. When I'd see him live, standing on top of the guitar and pulling on the neck, I'd get sick. "Stevie, you're gonna break it!!" The neck got a little loose on that guitar, even when it was screwed down, so if I told him the guitar was a little out of tune, he'd just give the neck a *yank* and it would be right back to pitch.

GW How did you set up the band for *Couldn't Stand the Weather*?

MULLEN Chris' drums were in the big room, and Stevie's amps were in the larger iso [*isolation*] booth on the left; it had a sliding glass door. The door was left open some of the time, even though he played so loud the guitar sound bled into the drum mikes. This wasn't that much of a problem, however, because most of his takes were keepers.

Depending on the song, he'd either stand right next to his amps or he'd leave the glass door open a little and stand in the big room with Chris. I think guitar players play better without headphones, because headphones can get in the way of their relationship with the instrument; they start to overpick because they aren't feeling it the same way. I always tried to allow Stevie to play without headphones, because, this way, he would be just as animated in the studio as he was in his live performances. He dance around, slidin' across the room on his toes, stuff like that.

GW Did he use any different amplifiers this time?

MULLEN It was exactly the same, except he had his own Dumble, the 150-watt Steel String Singer, by that point. The first time Stevie ever heard his Dumble was when it came into Texas Music, some time before we went up to the Power Station. It was sitting on a bench in a 12-by-10-foot room, plugged into a 4x12 cabinet, and he had it cranked! It sounded like the biggest thing on the planet. He hit the low E and it was like God just showed up! [*laughs*]

But Stevie didn't understand why it sounded different in a big room, where the sound pressure wasn't enveloping your entire body. When we starting working on the second record, he came in the control room and said, "My Dumbles don't work anymore. They don't sound right!" So we'd try a hundred different things, but we'd always end up with the exact same thing, which was the 4x12 Dumble bottom, the Dumble top and two Fender Vibraverbs, every time.

When we were getting ready to record "Voodoo Chile," I was turning the knobs on his amp while he was playing, and I know I lost some hearing that day; it was so loud, and I was trying to get the tone and the distortion level just right. That was probably the loudest thing I ever heard in my life.

GW Did you use any ambient miking on the guitar tracks?

MULLEN There was no need to, because the takes were pretty live and the drum mikes were picking up some of the room sound. But too many mikes create phase cancellation problems. You'll get a fatter, thicker tone with less microphones.

GW Was "The Sky Is Crying" recorded during the sessions for *Couldn't Stand the Weather*?

MULLEN Yes. "The Sky Is Crying" was one of my favorite songs that Stevie played, and I pushed him to record it during the *Couldn't Stand the Weather* sessions. He recorded it for the third record, *Soul to Soul*, too, but it didn't make either album [*the song was included on the posthumous release,* The Sky Is Crying]. What's unusual about the released version of "The Sky Is Crying" is that it's a comp: the instrumental track was recorded during *Soul to Soul*, but the vocal track was recorded during *Couldn't Stand the Weather*. The vocal had to be flown in line-by-line [*to make it line up with the backing track*].

GW Had he written "Couldn't Stand the Weather" before going into the Power Station?

MULLEN He wrote that during the preproduction period in Austin, along with "Scuttle Buttin'," "Stang's Swang" and "Honey Bee."

GW Among his early compositions, the track "Couldn't Stand the Weather" reveals more diverse influences, from the soul/R&B bass line to the Hendrix vibe of the rhythm part to the Albert King–style soloing. It's much more rock oriented than any of the *Texas Flood* material.

MULLEN Stevie's biggest influence was the blues, but he started relying more on his own instincts at this point. I think Stevie made a decision that he didn't want to make the same kind of record as the first one. "Voodoo Chile" is a good example: it's a song they'd been doing live for a few years; it's not like they worked it up just for that record. And I pushed him to record it, because when he played "Voodoo Chile" live he brought a *life force* to the song that no one else possibly could.

GW Stevie was able to tap into Jimi's spirit without sacrificing his own signature style and sound.

MULLEN Right. Stevie played "Voodoo Chile" with so much soul and so much spirit—he nailed every note and every nuance. That take was live from beginning to end, and it's seven minutes of pure guitar energy without a single miscue. It would be hard to find anyone that could play guitar *that way* without some sort of mistake here or there, but he blew right through it.

GW Something that made Stevie so unique was his combination of abilities: he could play with incredible fire, spontaneity and feeling, but he was so precise in his execution.

MULLEN Most guitarists that play with that kind of intensity and aggression have the tendency to rush, but Stevie's time was rock solid. He was the metronome of the band, which is what always amazed me. That fact that he could pull everything off with such precision is the very thing that allowed us to make the albums the way we did. Each take was based on Stevie's performance.

GW Did knowing he was capable of playing like this make it easier or harder to record him?

MULLEN He was a piece of cake to record. Until the time when Stevie slipped a little because of the drugs, there was a long period where he practically never missed a lick anywhere at any time. His performances were flawless—on *Austin City Limits,* live in concert, always. The only thing that was even mildly difficult was the vocal, because he sometimes had a tendency to oversing. But he had such a great voice, and he learned real quick how to deal with that.

GW What are your feelings today about *Texas Flood* and *Couldn't Stand the Weather*?

MULLEN In looking back at these two records, I would say that I like the second one a little more than the first. *Texas Flood* was Stevie's introduction to the world, but that's the Stevie I'd known for six years. He was just playing blues and shuffles, but of course he was playing it like no one had ever played it.

On *Couldn't Stand the Weather*, Stevie was coming into his own and branching out into things that were more ambitious. Lincoln Clapp came up to me during the *Couldn't Stand the Weather* sessions and said, "You did such a great job on *Texas Flood*—everything is so consistent." And I laughed and said, "No wonder. Because in the two hours it took to cut it, not a knob was moved!"

I would never have been involved with Stevie if I didn't have my own passion for what he was doing. I did those soundchecks in the early days because it was *his* gig, and I wanted to be there. I've always loved his playing so much.

[12]

"It was one of those gigs where you see someon and **you can't believe wh** you're hearing."

—*JIMMIE VAUGHAN*

GONE HOME

An inside look at Stevie Ray Vaughan's
final performance on August 26, 1990,
in East Troy, Wisconsin.

STEVIE RAY VAUGHAN WAS right where he wanted to be as midnight approached on August 26, 1990. Earlier that evening, he had closed out a triumphant summer tour with Double Trouble, opening for Eric Clapton, one of his heroes, in front of a sold-out crowd of 30,000 at the Alpine Valley Music Theatre, just outside of East Troy, Wisconsin. Now, as Clapton's show was drawing to a close, the guitarist called Vaughan back out for a final encore performance of the blues standard "Sweet Home Chicago." Joining them onstage was the night's first performer, Robert Cray, along with two more of SRV's heroes: Buddy Guy and big brother Jimmie Vaughan.

Stevie Ray was all smiles as the five guitarists took turns soloing throughout the lengthy jam. Almost four years after cleaning up and leaving alcohol behind, the Texas guitarist was on top of his game. *Family Style,* his new album with Jimmie, was in the can, due to be released in another month. The feuds that had separated the brothers were long buried.

The show was the second of a two-night stand, and Stevie's playing was, by all accounts, fiery and fresh. With his favorite guitarists surrounding him, it must have felt to him like the exclamation point on a fantastically productive and happy period of his musical life.

"Those shows were just great fun, really exciting," recalls bassist Tommy Shannon. "They were sort of the culmination of all the good times we'd been having for the last year or two. And as good as we had been playing, those two shows were just unreal."

"As good as we had been playing, those two shows were just unreal."
—*TOMMY SHANNON*

Adds Jimmie Vaughan, "Stevie just *smoked.* It was one of those gigs where you see someone play and you can't believe what you're hearing. Stevie was unreal. He was just on another plane, and we all knew it."

When the final jam finished to an ecstatic roar at about 12:15 A.M., the musicians left the stage through a rear exit. Backstage, Clapton and Vaughan reportedly talked about paying tribute to Jimi Hendrix with some future gigs. Stevie, 35, was supposed to drive back to Chicago with Jimmie and Jimmie's wife, Connie, but then he heard that he could hop onto one of Clapton's four waiting helicopters. He initially thought all three of them could hitch this ride. When he learned that there was only one spot, he asked Jimmie and Connie if they minded if he grabbed it. "I really want to get back," he explained.

The Bell 206 B helicopter took off in fog around 12:40 A.M. with Vaughan and four others aboard and almost immediately slammed into the middle of a nearby manmade ski slope, killing all aboard.

They were just over half a mile from the venue but no one heard the crash, and a search for the wreckage wasn't begun until 5 A.M. At around 7, searchers found the bodies of Vaughan, pilot Jeff Brown and three of Clapton's associates.

"In the blink of an eye my life was taken away from me."
—*TOMMY SHANNON*

"I was woken up by a phone call from our tour manager saying that we had to have a meeting in my room right away," Shannon recalls. "A few minutes later I got a call from our manager, saying that one of the helicopters had gone down, Stevie was on it, and there were no survivors. In the blink of an eye my life was taken away from me." Double Trouble drummer Chris Layton got the news from Shannon. Says Shannon, "I was sitting on the bed crying, and Chris came into my room, asking what was going on. I said, 'Stevie's dead,' and he just lost it, too."

Adds Layton, "I was in denial and didn't believe it at all, so I called security and forced them to let me into Stevie's room. I really thought he'd be laying there sleeping, but when they opened the door, the bed was still made, the pillow turned down, with mints laying on it, and I just realized, My God, it's true.

"I felt like a baby, just completely helpless. Then we realized that the news reports said that Stevie *and his band* were killed, and

I realized that I had to get a hold of family and tell them that I'm still alive."

Clapton and Jimmie Vaughan were called and asked to identify the bodies. Over 1,500 people attended SRV's memorial service in Dallas. He is buried at Laurel Land Memorial Park in South Dallas.

[13]

The world is stunned, but
the people of Austin
are crushed.

THE SKY IS CRYING

Nowhere was the loss of Stevie Ray Vaughan
more keenly felt than in the cities
of Austin and Dallas.

BY BILL MILKOWSKI

MONDAY, AUGUST 27—AUSTIN

THE FIRST FLASH COMES over the Associated Press wire at about seven A.M.: "Copter crash in East Troy, Wisconsin. Five fatalities, including a musician."

Keen-eyed staffers at the Austin *American-Statesman* catch that item and begin putting two and two together. The AP updates its story every half hour with fresh details: The mysterious "musician" soon becomes "a member of Eric Clapton's entourage"—and then, "a guitarist." By 9:30, rumors spread that Stevie Ray Vaughan, Austin's favorite son, was aboard the doomed craft.

At 11:30 A.M., Clapton's manager confirms the worst: Vaughan

Editor's note: This article contains passages that appear elsewhere in this book.

was indeed among the passengers in the five-seat helicopter, which slammed into a fog-shrouded hillside near southeastern Wisconsin's Alpine Valley ski resort. Stevie Ray had boarded the aircraft after performing in an enormous blues show at the resort, and taken part in an all-star finale/jam on Robert Johnson's "Sweet Home Chicago." The program and the jam featured Stevie Ray, Eric Clapton, Robert Cray, Jimmie Vaughan and Chicago blues legend Buddy Guy, all of whom ripped it up before an ecstatic crowd of 25,000.

Four Bell 260B Jet Ranger helicopters awaited the artists and their respective entourages following the jam. Because of poor traffic conditions at Alpine Valley—only one two-lane road leads from the venue, and gridlock delays of an hour or more are common—major acts usually depart via helicopter.

The caravan of blues stars departed from Alpine Valley at two-minute intervals. The first, second and fourth copters landed without incident at Chicago's Meigs Field. The third, bearing members of Clapton's entourage and Stevie Ray, never made it. Poor visibility due to dense fog is prominent among factors blamed for the disaster. (The Austin *American-Statesman* later reports that Federal Aviation Administration records show that the pilot, Jeffrey William Brown, had two previous helicopter accidents.)

By noon, the capital city of Texas is in a state of deep shock. Stevie Ray's death is the most devastating blow to the Lone Star State's music community since Lubbock's Buddy Holly, along with Richie Valens and the Big Bopper, went down in an Iowa plane crash 31 years earlier. Residents who knew Stevie Ray walk about tearfully, dazed and disoriented.

"I've been calling people I haven't talked to in 15 years," says Austin singer-songwriter Natalie Zoe. "Everyone has been reaching out and trying to make connections with people who knew how important Stevie was to them. I mean...he was our homeboy."

By five P.M., merchants have posted signs and hoisted banners proclaiming "We Love You Stevie" and "So Long Stevie" outside their stores. Even the Holiday Inn replaces the cheery "Welcome Conventioneers" adorning its marquee with a somber "SRV R.I.P." Plumbing stores, Tex-Mex restaurants, musical instrument stores, donut shops—all fly the flag of grief in this central Texas town, where Little Stevie Vaughan, the skinny kid from Oak Cliff, became Stevie Ray Vaughan, hometown hero and Austin's musical ambassador to the world.

Fans begin converging on Zilker Park, where, 10 years earlier, mourners gathered for a candlelight vigil on the night John Lennon was murdered. Now they sit side-by-side in the darkness, with 3,000 points of light flickering in a sea of sorrow. Tattooed Chicano bikers, lawyers in Brooks Brothers suits and crystal-wielding New Agers spread out on blankets and meditate in silence. Fans clutching photos of SRV construct shrines to the fallen guitar hero. Young gunslingers tote their Strats, Buddhists chant and old friends weep openly as disc jockey Jody Denberg of Austin's KLBJ radio pumps a steady stream of SRV through a makeshift P.A. The sound of Stevie Ray's stinging Strat pierces the night air and the hearts of the huddled blues fans, offering bittersweet solace to the bereaved.

"It's depressing and spiritually healing at the same time," says one SRV fan, who clutches an autographed copy of *Texas Flood* he'd received from the guitarist some years earlier.

Even as the mourners gather at Zilker Park, others instinctively head to the club Antone's, a focal point of the Austin blues scene throughout the mid Seventies and a favorite hangout of the Vaughan brothers over the years. Some fans have driven from as far as Oklahoma to be here in honor of Stevie Ray; others come on foot from their dorms on the campus of Texas University, listening to disc jockey Paul Ray's "Blue Monday" tribute on KTU as they walk. One fan fondly recalls the night in 1978 when Stevie Ray went toe-to-toe on stage at Antone's with Otis Rush, the great left-handed bluesman who wrote "Double Trouble," the tune after which SRV named his band. Another mourner describes the night he saw Little Stevie play with Albert King in 1975. A younger fan relates, in still-awed tones, his excitement over witnessing a 1987 jam that saw Stevie Ray and Jimmie joined by U2's The Edge and Bono.

Local TV stations begin converging on the club by nine P.M. Their cameras and microphones focus on SRV intimates, such as club owner Clifford Antone, a close friend to both Vaughan brothers.

"I met Stevie when I was 22 and he was 17," he sobs. "The kid could always play. I mean, he could play as good then as he does now. People like that...it's just born in 'em, you know? He was Little Stevie back then, just a kid. He'd hang out and play and make you laugh. It was a very simple thing. It had nothing to do with the record business, or TV or movies or any of that shit. Him, me, Jimmie, Denny Freeman, Doyle Bramhall...we were all just a bunch of kids, drawn together by our love for the blues, you know? And even in recent years, when I'd see him, I'd say, 'How ya doin', kid?' I mean, he was my friend, just this little guy who played guitar. The rest is the world's trip, you know?"

It is somehow appropriate that WC Clark is booked this night at Antone's. A black bluesman from East Austin, WC played with Stevie Ray and singer Lou Ann Barton in the late-Seventies band Triple Threat Review. Last year, the three were reunited for a special Austin City Limits program that celebrated WC's 50th birthday.

"I'm dumbfounded," says Clark, appearing quite shaken. "He was an easygoing person, really lovable. I felt like a benefactor to him."

TUESDAY, AUGUST 28—AUSTIN

STILL REELING FROM THE NEWS, the city tries to carry on. By now, every daily newspaper in the country has run some kind of front page item about the tragic loss. The world is stunned, but the people of Austin are crushed—still shaking their heads in disbelief, wondering aloud, Why? Why now, after he had cleaned up and gotten his life back together?

Old friends and colleagues show up at Antone's this night, to hug each other and help brush away the tears that won't quit. Doug Sahm, David Grissom, Paul Ray, Little David Murray, Derek O'Brien, Van Wilks, Marcia Ball and dozens of other Austin notables take the stage and play for Stevie Ray. And they recall both the lean years and the good times.

Natalie Zoe remembers Stevie Ray as the nice guy who lived across the street in a funky, shack-ratty house on Thornton Road, near the railroad tracks. "We were all young and broke back in the late Seventies," she says. "None of us on that street had any air conditioning, and it was hot eight months a year. So we did a lot of hanging out on porches, picking guitars and trying to stay cool. I was playing steady gigs then, and he used to help me haul my gear out of the house and into my car. He was always very gentlemanly, very neighborly. Just a nice, sweet guy."

Eddie Munoz, an old friend of Stevie's, who played guitar in the early-Eighties band the Plimsouls, recalls SRV's uncanny ability to communicate directly through his instrument. "Stevie was a rarity. There are very few people who have that much soul and that much power, who can command so much attention just by plugging in a guitar. I remember one time, a couple of years before he got signed, I was on tour with the Plimsouls and ran into him in New Orleans. We were hanging around the French Quarter, and we walked into this open-air club; a blues band was playing. There were only three people in the audience, and Stevie Ray had his guitar with him, so the band let him sit in. And within five minutes, man, there was a crowd of a hundred people milling around outside, staring at this guy piping out this hot stuff on guitar. It was wild, man. The guy could always draw crowds by plugging that thing in. But he didn't carry any big pretense about it. He used to say to me, 'I don't know where it came from. It just happened. My brother Jimmie showed me some stuff, and then it was like the dam broke.'

"He was a great guy and a decent human being," Munoz continues. "He was just so shy and unassuming—until you put a guitar in his hands. He lived for playing that guitar. Everybody's jaw dropped whenever he played. There are those people who are just so blessed— one person out of millions who can touch the instrument and have it sing for him. He always had that."

Guitarist Van Wilks remembers SRV as someone who commanded respect from all the various musical cliques around Austin. "You had all these factions here in the early Eighties—the Antone's straight blues scene, the country scene, the New Wave college scene, the younger hard rock and heavy metal scene. But Stevie was able to transcend all of that, and without even being aware of it. He was..."

Wilks becomes aware of his use of the past tense, and freezes in mid-sentence. He hangs his head, and in a hushed tone, as if the life had just run out of him, says, "Man, it just now hit me."

WEDNESDAY, AUGUST 29—AUSTIN

A YOUNG MAN WITH shoulder-length blond hair slowly guides his wheelchair through the Austin airport terminal. He wears a Stevie Ray Vaughan T-shirt and a baseball cap sporting the striking David Coleman–designed SRV logo that adorns the *In Step* album cover. He looks confused and disoriented, lost in a sea of bustling Texas businessmen. He notices my long hair, and accurately sizing me up as a brother in SRV, wheels over to talk. Without any preamble he asks, "Hey, man, where's the funeral?" He's Doug Castor, a 33-year-old fan who has made the pilgrimage to Austin from Pittsburgh. Like other fans from around the country, he wrongly assumed that Stevie Ray was born here. In a musical sense, of course, Stevie Ray was born in Austin, and the town certainly adopted him. But I inform him that the funeral will be held Friday, at noon—in Dallas.

"Dallas?! Shit! How'm I gonna get to Dallas?!" With that, he spins his chair 180 degrees and wheels over to the Avis desk, where he inquires about handicapped-equipped rental cars. "I really can't afford this," he tells me, "but I just gotta be there. His music touched me in an important way."

That night at the Steamboat, another Austin guitar hero, Eric Johnson, dedicates his set to Stevie Ray. It is another cathartic act in a town coming to grips with cold, harsh reality.

THURSDAY, AUGUST 30—DALLAS

EN ROUTE TO A candlelight vigil in Oak Cliff, I tune in KNON-FM to catch disc jockey Dan O's tribute. "Here's some live Stevie Ray, recorded last year in Dallas with Robert Cray," he mutters in funereal tones, pausing a few seconds before adding, "...the last solo is screaming."

I pull into a park in the South Dallas neighborhood where Stevie Ray grew up. A red pickup truck with the words "Life without You" emblazoned in white paint on the hood informs me that this is the right place. I walk toward a thicket of many flickering lights. In the distance, in the middle of a grassy meadow, a few hundred mourners sit in a circle around a huge tree. Dozens of white candles placed around the tree trunk bathe the sad faces in an eerie glow. This is no beer-guzzling, carousing hang. The mood is respectful, peaceful. Their heads bowed, some mourners hold hands in silence as the flames illuminate a series of photographs placed at the base of the great tree.

Among the pictures is a telling shot of a 15-year-old Little Stevie playing a guitar. Same posture, same attitude—even then he had "The Look." Vigil organizer Christian Brooks speaks softly of growing up with Stevie and Jimmie in Oak Cliff. A part-time drummer and full-time custom leather craftsman (he made the strap worn so proudly and for so long by Stevie Ray), he recollects a true blue friendship that began at Kimball High and continued through the years.

Suddenly, the reverential silence is shattered by a man overcome by grief. He steps into the ring of mourners, shaking as he testifies: "I grew up with Stevie Ray. And I just wanna say that I loved Stevie Ray Vaughan." He begins meekly, but gains courage and conviction at the urging of the crowd. "Now, if you don't mind, I'd like to sing a song for him." The mourners shout their approval. He closes his eyes, summons some inner reserve, and belts out a psalm with sanctified intensity. Several in the crowd, tears streaming down their faces, raise their hands to the sky and praise God.

FRIDAY, AUGUST 31—DALLAS

MORE THAN 3,000 of the faithful gather at Laurel Land Memorial Park, braving 100-degree temperatures to say farewell to Stevie Ray. By noon those wearing suits are already drenched in sweat. Inside the chapel, close friends and family mourn in private. Outside, anxious photographers from AP, UPI and the local papers stand ready with telephoto lenses, waiting to snap the processional as it exits the chapel and moves the 100 yards or so to the site of the public service—near Stevie Ray Vaughan's grave. Cable networks and local TV stations are present in full force, their on-air crews trying to hold up under the intense heat.

Near the burial site are the more than 150 floral arrangements that have been sent from around the world. Several are shaped like Stevie Ray's Strat and bear his SRV logo. Off to one side, a recent photo of Stevie Ray is propped on an easel; his trademark black bolero is draped over one corner of the portrait. Nearby stands a placard: "We will cherish what you have given us and weep for the music left unplayed."

First to emerge from the chapel is Stevie Wonder. A hush comes over the crowd as he is led to a sheltered reviewing stand near the grave. The casket is placed in a white hearse, which slowly drives to the site; the mourners follow behind on foot. Jimmie and his mother, Martha, walk with the late guitarist's fiancé, Janna Lapidus. Strolling behind them, heads bowed, are Chris Layton, Tommy Shannon and Kim Wilson. Behind them are Jeff Healey and his band, a tearful

Charlie Sexton, Dr. John, ZZ Top's Billy Gibbons, Dusty Hill and Frank Beard, Mark Pollack of the Charley's Guitars store in Dallas, Colin James and Charlie Comer, Stevie Ray's personal friend and publicist for the past eight years. Buddy Guy, overcome with grief, slips out of the chapel into a nearby car.

The Reverend Barry Bailey of the First United Methodist Church of Fort Worth (Stevie Ray's AA sponsor) opens the service with some personal thoughts, his rich voice booming through two huge stacks of speakers. "We're here to thank God for this man's life," he begins. "He was a genius, a superstar, a musician's musician. He captured the hearts of thousands and thousands of people. I am thankful for the impact of this man's influence on thousands of people in getting his own life together in the name of God."

Bonnie Raitt, Jackson Browne and Stevie Wonder lead the crowd in a sing-along of "Amazing Grace."

Stevie Ray's close friend Bruce Miller steps to the podium and reads the "Twelve Steps to Recovery" from the Alcoholics Anonymous Big Book, placing it on the casket as he concludes. Several mourners weep openly as Nile Rodgers eulogizes Stevie Ray by recalling a tune from the *Family Style* session he had produced only a few short weeks earlier:

"In the song 'Tick Tock,' he sings the refrain, 'Remember.' And what Stevie was trying to tell all of us was, 'Remember my music. Remember how important music is to all of us. And just remember that it's a gift.' Stevie was truly touched by the hand of God. He had a powerful gift. And through his music, he can make us all remember things that are very, very important, like love and family."

His voice begins to crack with emotion as he continues. "Jimmie and Stevie made me a part of their family when we were doing the record. And I feel very, very sorry that I wasn't able to say to Stevie, to his face, 'Thank you, Stevie. Thank you for making me remember music, thank you for sharing a part of your music with me. Thank you for sharing your love with me. Thank you for making me a part of your family. Thank you for making me your brother. I'll always love you. I'll always cherish the moments that we spent together. And believe me Stevie, I'll always remember.'"

With that, the soulful sound of Stevie's soothing vocal on "Tick Tock" begins to pour through the speakers, touching hearts and raising goose bumps. The crowd applauds and cheers as one.

Bonnie Raitt, Jackson Browne and Stevie Wonder lead the crowd in a sing-along of "Amazing Grace." Bonnie carries the melody as the other two harmonize. When Raitt says, "Take it, Stevie," the magnificent Wonder voice, swooping and swirling around the notes with awesome, emotionally charged power, causes many in the crowd to lose control. Tears flow as his voice soars.

Finally, the mourners line up. One by one they pass the casket, some tossing flowers, religious artifacts and guitar picks as they go by. The last to pay his respects is Doug Castor, the young man who had mistakenly flown in to Austin from Pittsburgh two days earlier. He wheels himself up to the casket and says his fond farewells to Stevie Ray Vaughan.

Back at the hotel, I lie quietly on my bed, listening to a tape of an interview I had with Stevie Ray in 1988, some months after his departure from the rehab center in Marietta, Georgia. His words still ring in my ears:

"There's just a lot more reasons to live now. I can honestly say that I'm really glad to be alive today, because, left to my own devices, I would've slowly killed myself. There were a lot of things I was running from, and one of them was me. But you can't run from yourself. It may sound kind of trite, like 'No matter where you go, there you are.' But it really is true. I've made a commitment now, not for the rest of my life, but just for today. Now, each day's a new victory."

[14]

ery time I heard Stevie play, I got chills

I knew I was in the presence of greatness.

—ERIC CLAPTON

SONG SUNG BLUE

On a blues night to remember, Eric Clapton,
B.B. King, Bonnie Raitt, Buddy Guy, Robert Cray
and other stars joined Jimmie Vaughan
in paying tribute to their late friend
and brother, Stevie Ray Vaughan.

BY ALAN PAUL

JIMMIE VAUGHAN IS ALL over the stage, teaching Eric Clapton vocal cues even as he demonstrates a slinky riff for Bonnie Raitt, Robert Cray and Buddy Guy. The super-group begins to run through a song, falling effortlessly into a deep, wide groove, when Clapton, a smile spreading across his usually stoic face, suddenly stops playing. The music trails off as, one by one, the musicians follow Clapton's gaze across the room.

B.B. King, the focus of this show-stopping attention, strides purposefully across the floor. Trailed by a guitar-case-toting valet, he ascends the stage and, like the father of the bride at a big, joyous wedding, embraces everyone in an expansive hug. He holds Vaughan in his arms a bit longer than the others, patting him three times on the back.

The valet takes Lucille out of her case and hands the guitar to King, who leans against a stool and begins to noodle away, loosening his fingers. Clapton respectfully takes a seat on a Fender Bassman directly behind B.B., as does Guy, both of them gazing reverentially at the blues patriarch.

When rehearsal resumes, it's with a new vigor. The circle is complete. The Godfather has arrived. The event has been stamped with the good blueskeeping seal of approval.

Vaughan, King, Clapton, Guy and Co. are all old friends, and their presence here is, in fact, a spectacular act of friendship. They have come to Austin, Texas, from near and far to pay tribute to their fallen comrade, Stevie Ray Vaughan, who died five years ago after participating in a similar summit meeting at Alpine Valley, Wisconsin.

The Austin show, organized and hosted by Stevie's brother, Jimmie, was held May 11 in a TV studio before an invitation-only crowd of 400 and videotaped for a future television broadcast; negotiations with several networks are currently under way. An album and home video will likely follow. The lineup included everyone who shared the stage with Stevie Ray on August 26, 1990, the guitarist's final night on earth—Clapton, Guy, Cray, and Jimmie Vaughan—along with King, the slide diva Raitt, and two New Orleans keyboardists who were close with Vaughan, Dr. John and Art Neville.

"It was easy to figure out who to ask," Jimmie said before the show. "These people were Stevie's heroes and his friends. Without them, there was no tribute.

"Doing this has been in the back of my mind for a long time, but I didn't want to do it too soon—I couldn't have handled it, and I wanted it to be far enough removed that it could be a happy event, and not just sad. Most importantly, I wanted the music to be natural, because I knew that's what Stevie would have wanted."

The musical mix was, in fact, so natural that the whole event seemed more like a college reunion than a show biz extravaganza. Displays of ego were non-existent—at least in the musicians' dealings with one another—and the artists seemed to relish their opportunity to play together. This was especially evident at rehearsals held the afternoon of the show, where spontaneous jams often broke out between takes and the arrival of every participating musician triggered a mini-celebration.

"We don't see each other near as much as we'd like," Vaughan commented, "and certainly not all together. This is really a treat."

Although rehearsal time for the concert was limited, songs came together almost instantly. King, whose regal arrival occurred less than three hours before showtime, worked out "Telephone Song"— which he had never sung before—in 45 minutes, twice stopping run-throughs to hear a playback of Stevie Ray's version (from *Family Style*) on a hand-held recorder.

"I just got the tape a week ago," he explained after the show. "I just hummed through it a couple of times and tried to learn the song and figure out how I would sing it. I never even thought about the guitar part. I just tried to hear the chord progression and come up with something to play. That's how you do it; you just get in and see what you got. I really like the song, but I didn't even think about what Stevie played."

That was how Jimmie wanted it. "I told everyone that I wanted them to play like themselves," Vaughan said. "You don't ask B.B. King or Eric Clapton to do anything else, and besides it wouldn't be the right way to honor Stevie. And the only reason this whole thing is happening is because we all love Stevie. That's why I organized it, and that's why all these people came to do it."

Vaughan's sentiments were echoed by the other performers, each of whom recalled personal memories of Stevie Ray. Clapton noted that his relationship with Stevie was fogged by chemical dependency; the first time they met, he recalled, he was still in the grips of alcoholism. At their second meeting, it was Stevie Ray who was battling the demons of substance abuse. The third time, they were finally in a clear-headed position to appreciate and discuss one another's talents.

"I didn't get to see or hear Stevie play near often enough," Clapton said. "But every time I did, I got chills and I knew I was in the presence of greatness. He seemed to be an open channel and music just flowed through him. It never seemed to dry up."

"The most lasting memory I have of Stevie is his passion," said Raitt. "I don't think there's anyone who tears into a song the way he did. I think Stevie Ray was coming from some place so deep and so beautiful that there's no one you can compare him to."

Still, no one other than B.B. King was prepared to make some comparisons, placing Stevie in the rarefied company of two of jazz's greatest innovators.

"When most of us play a 12-bar solo, we play maybe two choruses and the rest is all repetition," King said. "Stevie Ray was one of just a handful of musicians I've heard in my life—Charlie Parker and Charlie Christian come to mind—who weren't like that. The longer they played, the better they played. More ideas continuously happened. And that's the way Stevie was; his playing just flowed. He never had to stop to think.

"His execution was flawless, and his feeling was impeccable. He could play as fast as anyone, but no matter how fast he played, he never lost that feel. His guitar was his means of speech, and he spoke beautifully. I would say you could feel his soul. I know I did."

Buddy Guy, sitting at King's side, added simply, "He was one of the best ever. Period."

"That's right," King said. "He was a leader in what he did. Not a follower—a leader."

"I'm glad we're doing this," Guy continued. "And I'm glad we waited almost five years. I couldn't have even talked about it right afterward. He was like family to me; when he died, I felt as bad as if I had lost my kid. And I still can't believe he's not here anymore. But he wouldn't have wanted it to be sad, because this is about the music, and he loved the music so purely."

THE CONCERT WAS DIVIDED into two segments, the first featuring Stevie Ray's Double Trouble—bassist Tommy Shannon, drummer Chris Layton and keyboardist Reese Wynans, with additional support from guitarist/pianist Denny Freeman—and the second, Jimmie's Tilt-A-Whirl Band, with Freeman, drummer George Rains and organist Bill Willis, supplemented by Shannon.

Jimmie Vaughan kicked the show off with a blistering attack on "Texas Flood," the Larry Davis song which helped launch Stevie's career. Head down, Strat capoed at the third fret, Jimmie played with searing intensity, all serious business. His trademark pompadour in glorious, Brylcreemed form, Jimmie stretched out, playing more extended lines than is his wont. Raitt followed with a foot-stomping romp through "Pride and Joy," turning in a limber, fluid, yet biting, slide solo with a down-and-dirty distorted tone. Next up was Robert

Cray, who led the band through a distinctly Chuck Berry–flavored "Love Struck Baby," with Vaughan playing dead-on double-stops behind him. Dr. John followed with a sinuous, barrelhouse take on "Cold Shot," banging out his trebly triplets and octave bass lines with gusto.

Guy, taking the stage with one of his trademark polka-dot Strats, seemed genuinely moved, and several times appeared as if he might cry. "I felt Stevie looking down when I was playing," the guitarist explained after the show. Guy roared through his own "Mary Had a Little Lamb," which originally appeared on his *A Man and the Blues* album and was covered by Stevie Ray on *Texas Flood*. The always-unenviable task of following the hyper-magnetic Guy fell on Eric Clapton, who said simply, "I'm scared," before proffering a fairly straight rendition of "Empty Arms." Clapton tipped his hat to Stevie Ray with a few direct cops and several SRV-style neck-length glissandos.

The concert's second half began with B.B. King's first appearance of the night. Both King and his beloved Lucille were in fine form on "Telephone Song," offering up streams of melodic, liquid-toned guitar work. On the coda, rhythm guitarist Vaughan stepped forward, initiating some sterling interplay between two of blues guitar's most consummately tasteful players.

Raitt and Cray returned to the stage to duet on the rollicking "Hard to Be," each of them displaying the kind of hard-driving intensity that has been lacking in their own work of late. Cray's vocals dominated the mix, but while Raitt's singing may have been a tad tentative, her playing was remarkably sure-fingered, as she peppered the song with biting slide fills. On her solo, Raitt unwinded long, languid legato lines which glided over and around the hard-charging rhythm section.

Not to be outdone, Cray, eyes closed, stepped forward and released a handful of stabbing, staccato notes, which capped off a thoroughly impressive performance.

Clapton returned next, playing an inspired "Ain't Gone 'N' Give Up on Love." He grabbed the slow blues by the throat and shook it with feral intensity. Playing with fire in his belly and passion in his heart, Clapton unleashed a barrage of rapid-fire, increasingly aggressive licks on his cream-colored Strat. An impressively fiery performance.

Next to return to the stage was Guy. A mesmerizing singer, he turned "Long, Long Way from Home" into a dramatic, foreboding, vocal showpiece. Starting at low volume, Guy masterfully manipulated dynamics to build from a whisper to a roar, letting out a burst of barely controlled feedback which served as a perfect metaphor for his reckless playing, which, though it often seemed on the verge of falling apart (and occasionally did), kept the crowd riveted to every note. Predictably unpredictable, Guy was the only performer to radically deviate from that afternoon's rehearsal.

Art Neville sang a moving, churchy "Life without You," the lyrics taking on poignant new meaning in his rendition: "Oh, how I miss you...the angels have waited for so long, now they have their way... take your place...fly on, fly on, fly on my friend."

The concert was gaining steam, but the real fun was just about to begin, as everyone took the stage for the much-anticipated grand finale. Vaughan, standing at center stage, launched into "Six Strings Down," a moving tribute to his brother from his own *Strange Pleasure* album. Everyone kicked in, each player finding a corner of the song and making it his or her own, with Cray firing off economical, chiming counterpoint to Raitt's stinging slide, King playing fills to Clapton's slinky three-note solo figure, and Guy unleashing piercing, single-note bends to answer Vaughan, who fingerpicked the main theme on his battered Strat. The sounds rose together and meshed into one glorious guitar wail, sending the song soaring into the stratosphere.

And when Vaughan, head thrown back, eyes tightly clenched, sang "Alpine Valley, in the middle of the night/Six strings down, on the heaven-bound flight/Got a pick, a strap, guitar on his back/Ain't gonna cut the angels no slack/Heaven done called another blues stringer back home," the music was so powerfully evocative of Stevie Ray that for a lingering instant it seemed as if he might stride on stage, Number One Strat in hand. It was a transcendent moment—the kind one is lucky to experience a handful of in a lifetime of playing and listening to music.

"We all felt it," Jimmie Vaughan said after the show. "A really special moment passed between us all. That just happens sometimes in music. My mother and some other family and friends in the audience confirmed what I thought—they all felt it too."

But there was still much more to come. Vaughan's trio of backup singers took the stage for "Tick Tock," a paean to world peace and universal spirituality written by Jimmie and Nile Rodgers and sung by Stevie on *Family Style*. Mono-named singer Briz took the song to church, building a gospel fervor that was picked up on by King, who launched a soaring cluster of blue notes which ascended like a mournful lamentation for Stevie Ray. As the song built to a crescendo, with Clapton playing a pungent solo, Jimmie looked upward and grinned from ear to ear.

At the conclusion of "Tick Tock," an unrehearsed jam erupted, with King playing a flurry of his trademark, heavily vibratoed licks, which Cray answered with a pithy, sharp-toned attack. Guy responded with several overbends, so absurdly wide that they cracked up Clapton, who flashed a huge cross-stage grin at Vaughan. But Guy had only just begun; he unleashed a cluster of seemingly insane notes, entering a land of total abandon where few dare to tread. But Clapton took up the challenge, answering Guy with a chorus of repeats which built to an impressive, if more controlled, frenzy. Raitt responded with spitfire slide clarions, before Jimmie literally leapt to center stage, taking over with his own unorthodox attack—percussive, staccato fingerpicking.

The song was winding down, but no one was ready for the evening to end, so Clapton took another chorus, which B.B. answered, the two of them engaging in a call and response. Then, with the band laying out, the guitarists went round-the-clock playing unaccompanied choruses: Cray, King, Guy, Clapton, Raitt and Vaughan, a conversation between the six surviving members of blues' first family. And when it ended, the royalty still weren't quite ready to vacate the throne.

King stretched the night out for a few more glorious minutes by breaking into "When the Saints Go Marching In," evoking the spirit of a New Orleans funeral where, once the deceased is laid to rest, a marching band kicks into party mode, looking death in the eye and celebrating the beauty and delicacy of life. The song led to everyone taking another unaccompanied chorus, until the inevitable happened and this summit meeting was actually, finally, over. Hugs and handshakes broke out all over the stage. Jimmie went right for B.B., and the blues patriarch wrapped the bereaved brother in a giant bear hug at center stage as everyone crowded around and slapped their backs, joining in on a communal embrace. The evening was over, tribute had been paid. It was not hard to picture Stevie Ray Vaughan, somewhere, tipping his hat in thanks.

✳